I0412088

An Examination of Institutional Reform in South Carolina

An Examination of

Institutional Reform in South Carolina

A Qualitative Research Study

Ashley Krejčí-Shaw

An Examination of Institutional Reform in South Carolina by Ashley Krejčí-Shaw

© 2015 Ashley Krejčí-Shaw. All rights reserved. This material may not be reproduced, displayed, modified or distributed without the express prior written permission of the copyright holder. For permission, contact the researcher at:
ashley.krejcishaw@mail.sit.edu

Although every precaution has been taken to verify the accuracy of the information contained herein, the publisher assumes no responsibility for any errors or omissions. No liability is assumed for damages that may result from the use of information contained within.

ISBN-13:
978-1508436485

ISBN-10:
1508436487

This capstone paper is dedicated to my nephews and written in remembrance of children that endured abuses in South Carolina reformatories.

Table of Contents

Preface

How and why are African American boys in South Carolina (SC) disproportionately removed from school? In 2013, this was the first of many questions that directed my capstone inquiry to examine the institutional landscape in South Carolina.

My examination began when a colleague suggested I browse through juvenile delinquency data she was using for an educational grant. I was dispirited by the information she passed along and continued fact-finding to learn more about the state's institutional topography. All of this led to research and a capstone paper titled "An Examination of South Carolina's Institutional Reforms and Their Impact on the Self-Narratives of African American Men," which was submitted in July 2014 in partial fulfillment for a Master of Arts in Sustainable Development. On July 24, 2014, I fulfilled the final requirement in Brattleboro, VT by presenting my research to SIT Graduate Institute faculty and colleagues.

My experience in the field brought forth numerous chance meetings with institutionally displaced youth. Specifically, I credit the five young men that granted me in-depth interviews for providing invaluable narratives that merit thoughtful consideration. I extend my thanks to the staff at my practicum site for opening their doors to me, and to each person that shared their experiences candidly or at length on various topics.

My daily field experiences were documented through jottings and analytical memos at the end of each day. A recurring thread that emerged in my writing was structural inequality, and I often found myself referring to 'structural faults' as described by youth who had been removed from school. I did not have the time or latitude to explore all terms and concepts that emerged in great detail. Even so, the notion of structural inequality and fault lines was essential to my interpretation of historical data in relation to the present-day social realities observed in the field. I submit this term now to impart to readers that my research explores how institutional authority has impacted boys and men, as opposed to exploring questions that debate whether there has or has not been an impact.

In closing, I underscore this point because the paper clarifies historical variance regarding the beginning of criminal and juvenile reform; and, even more so, how it was enacted well beyond those beginnings. Currently, disproportionate rates of delinquency and school removal extend beyond nuances in disciplinary methods of authority. Within these pages, the ethical dilemma facing organizational bodies in South Carolina is confronted. In addition, this research champions the value of qualitative research in building new reconciliatory practices of reform.

Acknowledgements

I would like to acknowledge the guidance and support I have had on this journey: my husband, for his love and fidelity to my dreams; my parents for their encouragement and unwavering belief in me; and, additionally, my Godparents who generously opened their doors to me as I conducted field research.

I extend heart-filled thanks to SIT Associate Professor Dr. Teresa Healy. In fall 2013, I enrolled in the first course she taught at the Institute, titled *Practitioner's Inquiry*. During this course, I witnessed Dr. Healy's exceptional command of qualitative research, and it prepared for its real world application. I am also grateful to my capstone advisor Professor Nikoi Kote-Nikoi for accepting me as an advisee. I am a better-informed global citizen and development professional because of his economic expertise and artful instruction.

Abbreviations and Acronyms

SC	South Carolina
US	United States (of America)
GED	General Equivalency Degree
CSC	Construct, SC
CUS	Construct, USA
CRT	Critical Race Theory
SCDJJ	South Carolina Department of Juvenile Justice
DJJ	Department of Juvenile Justice
RNB	Reformatory for Negro Boys
SCISB	South Carolina Industrial School for Boys
SBCCSC	State Board of Charities and Corrections of South Carolina
SCSBPW	South Carolina State Board of Public Welfare
SCDOC	South Carolina Department of Corrections

Abstract

In the State of South Carolina (SC), African American male adolescents disproportionately face disciplinary action in public schools and other institutions.

In 2013, South Carolina's Department of Juvenile Justice (SCDJJ) released data that listed Black male children comprising 57% of all juvenile referrals in the state. This disproportionate trend is also present in South Carolina's correctional system. In 2013, South Carolina's Department of Corrections (SCDOC) reported that out of 20,777 male prisoners, 13,631 were Black.

For adolescents or young adults looking to continue their education, alternative programs are available. One program that captures educationally displaced children in South Carolina is "Construct, SC"[1] (CSC). It is one of four affiliate programs of a national non-profit, "Construct, USA"[2] (CUSA), that operates in the state. The research carried out considers the efficacy of one affiliate to deliver program outcomes and includes critical insights of the author working at that affiliate's program site.

The racial and correctional implications of school removal inform discussions on South Carolina's institutional framework in

---

[1] "Construct, SC" is a pseudonym for the affiliate program, and also researcher's practicum site.
[2] "Construct, USA" is a pseudonym for the federally funding national program

the lives of Black adolescents and young adults today. A critical theoretical approach is employed in this paper to examine the state agencies most prevalent in the lives of Black men, in a bid to ascertain how the observed disproportionate trends developed. The paper incorporates five interviews conducted with men enrolled in CSC. The interviews outline their experiences in public school, the juvenile justice and state corrections systems.

This paper argues that the structural inequalities that impact African Americans today correlate closely with those of South Carolina's slave-holding past. Indeed this history is the basis for the state's development and upkeep of its contemporary correctional culture and delinquency reform strategies against Black boys and men. Facilities that were established and in operation until the 1970s are understood to be at the epicenter of subsequent inter-generational societal and achievement deficits among Black men in the state.

Introduction

The question this research addresses is two-fold: (1) *how has the existing reform-culture emerged and come to dominate institutional frameworks in South Carolina, and (2) how has it impacted the self-narratives of young, adult African American males?*

This study seeks to identify and reaffirm the challenges experienced by young adult African American males working to meet their livelihoods and improve their life chances in the state of South Carolina. It attempts to illuminate the experiences of a small group of men enrolled with a non-profit known as (CSC), whose primary institutional objective is to support low-income youth (ages 16-24) in earning their general equivalency degree (GED) or industry standard trade certifications. The organization is recognized as a non-profit that seeks to transform the lives of its program constituents by providing educational opportunity, job training and trade certification. CUSA is considered one of three institutional bodies with a significant presence in the lives of African American males. It is regarded as an ambassador for other federally funded, reputable and longstanding non-profits that aim to uplift inner-city youth.

The CSC program is the foundation of this research study as many observations included in this paper relate to the affiliate or larger operations of the program site. Observations that I, the researcher, obtained brought forth questions that necessitated examination of the state's education and correctional institutions and how they impact adolescents in South Carolina, in contrast to non-profit organizations like CUSA and its over 40 affiliate programs throughout the US.

In the summer of 2013, I was accepted as a practicum student at the "Community Center"[3] located in Sumter County, South Carolina. The Center provides a variety of services and is located in a low-income part of town. It is an information hub utilized daily by younger and older generations who rely on the Center's staff to connect them with educational, job or housing resources. The Center receives some operational support as it is considered a department of

---

[3] "Community Center" is a pseudonym for the researcher's practicum site.

municipal government, but its operational lifeblood comes, in the main, through grants.

I worked closely with the Center's Director[4] to conduct an internal inquiry on her behalf. This was the second phase of my practicum, which was broken into two components over one year. She assured me that the assignment was already discussed with the staff and that she had asked staff members to provide their full cooperation. The Director cited concerns about internal operations that I found reasonable and were thus the reason for assigning the task. Essentially, she required a third party to initiate a dialogue with her CSC staff. In less than a year, communication between her and the staff had declined dramatically. This was of concern to the Director because she planned to retire within several months and hoped to iron out organizational kinks within CSC, which is the Center's most valuable and demanding program. I conducted six semi-structured interviews with Construct, SC and adhered to interview procedures including transcribing and coding to unravel the issues that became more apparent with each passing interview. I turned in a carefully written report to the Director and scheduled a presentation to report the analysis to the staff. I used great discretion in revealing the full scope of my findings, considering the terms of the assignment (and who assigned it). The expected outcome was to determine the cause of the staff not communicating with the Director

---

[4] Director is a pseudonym for executive director of the Community Center.

in order to improve overall operations and prepare for a change in leadership. The Director and I agreed that the wellness and betterment of the program required rebuilding a consensus with her staff.

In the context of my broader capstone research, I offer this experience because it led to an unexpected outcome: my interviews, discussions and observations involving CSC became a turning point in my research focus. The reflections written around the time of the interviews and thereafter describe a highly reflexive effort on my behalf to understand the nuances of the CSC program and its staff, mainly in relation to its program constituency. Around this time, the staff had enrolled a new group of young adults, yet communicated a frustration about the group they had only recently chosen. According to the staff, the group lacked motivation, seriousness, enthusiasm and appreciation for *their* hard work. More so, young adults exhibited few leadership skills, at least those that attended on a regular basis. As the Director remarked to me privately about her staff's frustrations, *why then did they select them for the program?*

Once my first assignment was complete, I asked the Director and the staff if I could spend time with the CSC program observing and participating for a week or so. Both the Director and staff encouraged me to do this and even asked that I share observations and facilitate activities if I chose to do so. The first week of participant observation did not yield similar opinions about the newly admitted CSC program participants. In fact, my impressions opposed the sentiments of the staff *almost* entirely. Thus, I was intrigued to understand more about how a seemingly well-intentioned staff could view their constituents in one way and I another. I might also mention that the Director at this time often questioned the opinions of her staff as well on the issue, meaning she did not share the same frustrations as the staff did. When given the opportunity to form my own assessment, I was able to realize the latitude and complexity of how their opinions formed.

Organization of Study

This study is organized so as to offer a clear organizational and historical context for understanding the complexities of race and class stratification uncovered at my practicum site, and their relevancy for my research question.

Having introduced some initial comments about the organizational context of the study, my third section offers a more detailed review, with illustrations, from the relevant scholarly literature. The intent of this section is to anchor my study in the 'critical race' perspective, and draw from a community of scholars who use various strands of Critical Race Theory (CRT) to identify and unravel some of the key hegemonic forces that have been at play at critical periods in South Carolina's history. Additionally, historical papers are reviewed to offer a first-hand institutional perspective on how, over time, a culture of control and reform came to develop in the state. This section also serves to ground the research in its use of CRT, as the operation of such reformatories are understood to be at the epicenter of subsequent inter-generational societal and achievement deficits.

The fourth section of the paper addresses *The Problem* as observed and experienced in South Carolina, includes an overview of public school segregation, stereotyping and prison culture in the state today. All are the subsequent result of classism, racism and for-profit schemes, mostly in agriculture, that resulted in the exploitation of labor amongst South Carolina's poor and Colored; Negro[5] men and boys were often targeted.

This culture assumed prevalence in the lives of African American males that originated in a multi-institutional manner around Reconstruction (1863-1877). It is a period known to many for the start of well-documented efforts by the white Southern establishment to re-establish or retain their economic and social power in response to new legal protections afforded to a newly freed African American populace.

Section six reports my *Findings,* and it is outlined in three parts. First, *Portraits* that are written narratives of the interviews conducted and transcribed. The second is *Researcher Analysis: Critical Statements and Reflection* that includes quotes that correlate to key discussions within the body of the paper and then analyzes why the statement or reflection is critical. The third part consists of tables constructed to better organize the interview data and organize the life experience shared by the men. However, they were used in my analysis and detail certain nuances such as vocal intonation, body language, repeated phrases, word repetition, etc.

---

[5] *Negro* and *Colored* is used interchangeably with *African American* and *Black* at times throughout the paper to reflect the historic use of the moniker, as other scholars included in the paper use them in similar fashion.

Review of the Literature

This review of the literature helps us identify trends in power relations between young, adult Black males and bodies of authority present in their lives from about five years of age until 18 years of age. There are many critical moments in the lives of the men interviewed that take place in an educational setting. For this reason, most of the literature reviewed includes discussion on public education, or its politicization. Public education is not only a significant institution, but is also shown to have considerable sway in the lives of the interview sample and other youth across the state. Furthermore, the racial implication of the sample's experiences requires the evaluation of CRT's utility to deconstruct this institutional system. The scholars included in the discussion below discuss hegemonic systems of power, modes of control, and the impacts on Black Americans being systemically marginalized during various periods and in various contexts throughout US history.

In South Carolina, at first look, the formation of a state agency like the South Carolina Department of Juvenile Justice (SCDJJ or DJJ) in the early 1900s seems influenced by efforts to segregate adolescents as most of society already was: based on skin color. The superiority maintained by the white southern establishment during this period should not be oversimplified merely as efforts to separate the races in a *White Black binary* (Leonard, 2012, p. 431). Rather, it was a post-slavery reevaluation and reintroduction of the physical and psychological abuses inflicted on the formerly enslaved, in new institutional guises such as the Reformatory for Negro Boys (RNB).

There are two institutions that formed in South Carolina to address adolescent needs or reform and they were the RNB and the South Carolina Industrial School for Boys (SCISB). However, there are conflicting dates on when exactly the RNB was established. SCDJJ notes that the state "Began its first statewide juvenile justice effort in 1893, when a wing of the state penitentiary was set aside as a *reformatory* for delinquent boys" (Trotti, 2014). If we value the agency's account of their own history, then we might also accept that this effort was exclusively for Negro boys (e.g., reformatory versus industrial school). According to Trotti, the RNB is formally on state record much later: "1907, the Reformatory for Negro boys was built on what would later become the Department of Juvenile Justice's Shivers Road facility," which is still located in Columbia, SC, (2014). This evidence reveals that South Carolina's juvenile delinquency began with Black males children 14 years before it is officially documented. More so, that the children were condemned to adult prisons and kept in 'reformatory' wings.

The second facility was established in 1910 for White children and was named Industrial School for Boys, or SCISB (Anderson, 2012). Thom Anderson is a South Carolina reporter that claims to have attended a high school that once neighbored the SCISB and states the White institution 'closed' when "juvenile justice institutions were desegregated in the 1970s" (2012).

Anderson's article[6] makes no mention of the RNB, but substantiates that an "industrial school for white boys" was approved by the state legislature in June 1906 (2012).

A handful of state agencies issued quarterly reports or special reports on health, education, war, corrections, and public welfare during this period. These reports affirm timelines, social characteristics, as well as the purpose and design of early juvenile reform in the state. One example is the *State Board of Charities and Corrections of South Carolina* (SBCC), an agency that reported on many matters of the state, including, most importantly, the operations of both institutions. The SBCC is noted as being superseded in 1920 by the State Board of Public Welfare, according to the digitalized reference note by HathiTrust Digital Library[7].

In 1915, the SBCC issued its first published report. In it, the SBCC describes disciplinary approaches used at the RBN as not dissimilar to those enforced generally by slave owners. The reformatory is explicitly described as being a jail, mandated to operate as a prison and to treat children as criminals. The annual report describes how they were treated in 1915:

> Other than Sunday school, which is conducted three times a
> month by the chaplain of the State Penitentiary [*Reformatory*

---

[6] Thom Anderson's original article was posted April 2010, but noted as being "updated" on *Friday, Dec 28, 2012.*

[7] The HathiTrust Digital Library *brings together the immense collections of partner institutions in digital form, preserving them securely to be accessed and used today, and in future generations* (HathiTrust.org).

for Negro Boys] and which the boys are required to attend, there are no educational facilities… Discipline is by confinement in barracks, shackling, and whipping. No parole system prevails. The Governor is the only channel through which parole for these boys can now be secured. The guards are armed with a shotgun and pistol. In a word, therefore, the Reformatory is operated on practically the same basis and principles that obtain at the State Penitentiary. It is not a reformatory, but a prison. (p. 73)

Determining the consequences of treating adolescent populations as criminals is key to establishing the ethnographic history of black males in South Carolina. This study includes no first-hand written or recorded accounts from Black or White children in narrative form – however – these could very well exist. Instead, this paper offers public documents written by observers of the abuses, which provides one account of the early institutional narrative. This narrative informs us on the political current that channeled Black boy children into structural gulfs of 'delinquent' detainment.

First, black male children were subject to vagrancy laws designed to jail African Americans-- South Carolina was one of nine states to implement vagrancy laws (Alexander, 2012). Vagrancy laws were Jim Crow tactics that "made it a criminal offense not to work…applied selectively to blacks" and furthermore "eight of those states enacted convict laws allowing for the hiring-out of county prisoners to plantation owners and private companies. Prisoners were forced to work for little or no pay" (Alexander, 2012, p. 28).

Three years after the first annual SBCC report and subsequently many quarterlies thereafter, the board and South Carolina's governor asked Dr. Hastings Hornell Hart to conduct a "War Program" study, as stated by the author in his report's prefatory note (Hart, 1918). Hart opens *The War Program of the State of South Carolina: A Report* to, "His Excellency, Richard I. Manning, Governor; the State Council of Defense; and The State Board of Charities and Corrections" as being in 'accordance' with their collect request to study the "social agencies and institutions of South Carolina as could be accomplished within the short period of two weeks," in which he submits the "facts" that he notes to have ascertained (Hart, 1918). Listed among his many visits were both the SCISB and RNB; the differences are stark. The SCISB is described as "A credit to the State. The boys are comfortably housed and well cared for" (Hart, 1918, p.42). More so, it is place of industry that produces enough "corn in its own mill and feeds it to its pupils in the form of corn meal or grits," (p.42). He writes that the boys wear neat khaki uniforms and the industrial and rudimentary training for the boys is well organized (p. 42). There is no mention of the young men as criminals, although we know it is a juvenile facility. Hart discusses the school's profitability and offers some cost-benefit analysis per boy, which he also notes as totaling 82. His main criticism is overcrowding of the dormitories and although he finds the double beds "objectionable" they were otherwise "clean, and comfortable and the boys were well cared for" (p. 42). The overcrowding, he added, was "pressure…temporarily relieved when the new building is opened" (p. 42).

Hart's description of the Negro Reformatory is far less impressive. He is far more detailed about the reformatory and on specific matters like the age of the children, and neglects otherwise basic operational details as outlined for the SCISB; in part because the operational procedures do not exist. Hart explicitly details:

> The boys are kept in a brick building, which is identical in its plan and construction with the prison buildings on the two farms for adult convicts. The part in which the boys are kept was bare, desolate, and dirty. The beds were dirty and uncomfortable. There was no heating apparatus except four smoky fireplaces in each of the two dormitories. The day was bitter cold and the boys were shivering around these fireplaces. There was no cooking apparatus, either ranges or steam cookers. All cooking had to be done in the brick ovens or in two large kettles. There was no laundry apparatus, but the boys washed their clothing, after a fashion, in ordinary washtub. There were no towels, toothbrushes or hairbrushes (p.43-44).

According to Hart, there are no funds appropriated to ensure adequate care of the boys who are, he states (twice) is comprised of boys between the ages of 7-12 years old (Hart, 1918, p. 44). He adds there is no provision for recreation and that when he inquired about what the Negro boys do for recreation, the superintendent told him

14

emphatically, "Farm work!" (p. 44). From what Hart describes, even if the Negro boys had opportunities for schooling or recreation there would be few resources available to them: "No school whatever, except a Sunday School, no library, no pictures, no writing materials… The only books found were a Bible… and some tattered illustrated Sunday school charts hung against a post, (1918, p. 43.)" There are many conclusions that can be drawn from Hart's assessment of the boys' living conditions and outlook, and there are significant economic implications as well. The children are essentially used as laborers and thus are the cheapest input at the state's disposal since slavery. The RNB contained *double* the number of juveniles, 190 boys as Hart affirms (p. 43). Consider Hart's description of the labor conditions and demands:

> All of the expenses for 190 boys have to be paid from the labor of the boys…Not only is this true, but last year in cotton picking time some of the boys were drafted from the Negro Reformatory to pick cotton on the other prison farms. The writer has visited perhaps 200 institutions for children, but only once before in his experience has he seen a company of children so utterly forlorn, miserable, and helpless as the boys in the Negro Reformatory of South Carolina (p. 43).

And the reasons for the "convictions" are cited by Hart as "burglary, larceny, assault, petty offences, shooting craps, and incorrigibility," and none which offer *any* justification - even considering the period – as to why the boys were treated so terribly (p. 43).

Thus far, there are two institutional sources that abridge inhuman treatment of African-Americans from an era of enslavement to a period Jim Crow. Uniquely, we are provided two different perspectives on the abuses of young males within three years. The SCBCC is written with no formal author, thus speaking as the institution purview in itself. On the other hand, Hastings Hornell Hart, whose extensive work on juvenile detentions centers seems long forgotten by Russell Sage Foundation[8], first offers sentiments of a *carpetbagger*[9] (McCord, 1914, p. 56). Hart's sympathetic tone is always remedied by his work objectives and often pivots to make the point that if the Negro adolescents continue to be treated horrifically they will continue to emigrate out of SC and subsequently be unavailable for future military duty (Hart, 1918).

Hart is jarred by his observations, but uncompelled to discuss the ethics or fiduciary responsibility of the state. It is again, about the adolescent Black boys' economic value and the risk or opportunity cost of overusing and abusing them now. When Hart wrote the 1918 "War Program" report, the First World War was in full swing and one reason why South Carolina emerged as a competitor in the textile industry. Many of South Carolina's poor worked for low wages or as we understand today, Negro labor allowed for greater profit margins because they had no rights to earn and could fulfill huge military contracts secured, (National Geographic News [NGN], 2010). Hart commends South Carolina for the moderate success of

---

[8] http://www.russellsage.org/search/node/Hastings
[9] *Carpetbagger* was a pejorative term used to describe the influx of White Northerners to the south during Reconstruction Era.

"employing" prisoners, because as he states the practice has increased the property value of convict farms and provided the state a net earning of "about $7,500 per year," (p 46). Hart's intention was not to embarrass his South Carolina employers by describing the conditions of the reformatory, but to stir them into rethinking their strategy for able-bodied Negro adolescents, should they be needed in the future; his final recommendation states:

Abolition of the county chain gain system and the transfer of the State Reformatory for Negro Boys from the control of the board of directors of the State Penitentiary to that of the board of trustees of the State Industrial School for Boys. These recommendations *seem radical,* but we believe that they should be adopted as a *practical war measure* (p. 48).

The underlying message is that altruism is a necessary practice in maintenance of a subordinate racial caste system. Altruism was demonstrated by the Freedman's Bureau during Reconstruction. Despite their mission as "The agency charged with the responsibility of providing food, clothing, fuel, and other forms of assistance to destitute former slaves," the Bureau failed in this mission (Alexander, 2012, p. 29). Civil Rights Attorney Michelle Alexander explores this period in US history and argues that a continuum of inequality and hostility mirrors that of what is known of post-Emancipation society. In her 2012 book *The New Jim Crow,* she posits an argument that the US penal system has disenfranchised millions of Black boys and men in a new era of mass correctional control. She reminds readers of two significant periods in US history in which the rights of black people broadened in the US: first, the Emancipation Proclamation issued in 1863, and the second being landmark Civil Rights legislation 100 years later. As Alexander (2012) affirms, the advancements of this period were 'extraordinary.' In her opening chapter "The Rebirth of Caste" she quotes W.E.B Dubois' famous quote about this period in US history: "The slave went free; *stood a brief moment in the sun*. Then moved back again toward slavery" (2012). As Alexander words it, "Sunshine gave way to darkness, and the Jim Crow system of segregation emerged— a system that put black people nearly back where they began, in a subordinate racial caste" (2012). Alexander elaborates in more historical terms:

> Prisoners were forced to work for little or no pay. One vagrancy act specifically provided   that "all free negroes and mulattoes over the age of eighteen" must have written proof of   a job at the beginning of every year. Those found with no lawful employment were deemed vagrants and convicted. Clearly, the purpose of the black codes in general and   the vagrancy laws in particular was to establish another system of forced labor. In W.E.B. Du Bois's words: "The Codes spoke for themselves ... No open-minded student can read them without being convinced they meant nothing more nor less than slavery in daily toil" (p.28).

The South Carolina Department of Corrections (SCDOC) indicates early agency misconduct on its website: "The *original* correctional system in South Carolina was established in

1866…1960, the Governor of South Carolina decided to end the abuses of the correctional system and therefore created a new state agency," (SCDOC, 2014). Recall, this was the same body that regulated the Reformatory for Negro boys until the 1970s, as noted by Anderson earlier. SCDJJ's website offers this overview of their agency history:

After the Civil War, the "Houses of Refuge" were replaced by larger state and city sponsored "Reform Schools," "Industrial Schools," and "Training Schools." South Carolina began its first statewide juvenile justice effort in 1893, when a wing of the state penitentiary was set aside as a "reformatory" for delinquent boys (Anderson, 2010).

The difference between the reform school and the industrial school are significant discussion points because despite being predicated with the same *intent* to reform, only one actually applied principles that we can associate with rehabilitation. The White children - whatever their "crime" and however serious - from all reports were trained, cared for and expected to move beyond whatever trespasses (if any) got them there. The reformatory, either by design to punitively punish males, or simply to exploit child labor, robbed generations of Black youth opportunities to develop into productive members of society; recall, the boys observed in the facility are described as 'hopeless' by Hart. The foggy agency histories never explicitly acknowledge that Black boys and adolescents were specifically targeted for labor. However, there is enough evidence to question and consider the extent of

19

intergenerational damage inflicted by the state based on what is documented.

Secondly, the advancement of rights for African Americans during this period unleashed an adversarial reaction that not only formulated Jim Crow, but domestic terrorist organizations to uphold structural assaults (e.g., Ku Klux Klan, lynch mobs). In the words of one Black retiree, a carpenter having lived and worked in Sumter County nearly his whole life, "They [RNB] got lots of them [Black boys]. For silly little things, real young too, maybe as young as seven, no, maybe nine [years of age]… But you see, they parents wouldn't usually take up for them," (C.L, personal communication, June 18, 2014). How many Black parents or their children were caught in the web of vagrancy? Historically, we know this to be many. More importantly, how many parents, or children for that matter, would have stood up to such aggression when confronting their Southern aggressors? Not many. Doing so would have meant showing contempt for White authority and as history also tells us, this could be dangerous and even result in death. Most importantly, Confederate resentment over the expansion of African American rights was rampant.

Michelle Alexander's book (2012) is subtitled "Mass Incarceration in the Age of Colorblindness." Her reasoning is all too clear in light of what the literature reviewed thus far has presented. Alexander notes that, "In the era of colorblindness, it is no longer permissible to hate blacks, but we can hate criminals" (p. 199). The concept and discussion of colorblindness is key in framing the problems commonly faced mostly by African American young adult males today, or at least in South Carolina. *Colorblindness* has yet to enter into the American mainstream with the same fervor as other terms and concepts. For instance, *anti-micro aggression* campaigns have popped up across the country and maybe for reasons not so different from why the *concept* of colorblindness is not *as* popular (McWhorter, 2014). Both terms speak to multiracial, multiethnic populaces that represent much of the US. However, microaggression is far more direct conceptually: person A asserts their identity to person B, thus (hopefully) enlightening person B and thus satisfying person A. Colorblindness also speaks largely to a multiracial, multiethnic populace, but its term is less clear. It suggests that we should *all be colorblind* because that would potentially allow everyone to treat one another equally and without a framework of racial bias. Conversely, *colorblindness* can be regarded as a way, at least as argued by Cornel West in the Foreword to Alexander's book, of trivializing black suffering. West's statement is key to understanding the challenges of young Black males today. As suggested by Dr. West, is intergenerational suffering trivialized? I have observed this to be true at my practicum site. It is also why the paper takes a panoramic view of South Carolina state agencies and literature up until the 1970s; it is an indictment that requires an extensive etiology. The implications of how colorblindness hinders race reconciliation are not just applicable to White and Black experiences. Mind you, this is how race is often understood in what many consider an orthodox *White Black binary*[10]. As Alexander suggests, we could date colorblindness back to the early practices of Jim Crow, as, again, a time in which it was acceptable to strip the rights of people deemed 'criminals' (2012, p.199).

Before sharpening the discussion to the definition of *race*, I backtrack to revisit one topic discussed in the introduction of this study: Construct, SC's *staff/constituent dynamics*. After participant observation supported my initial belief that the staff's criticism of the new group they accepted was, at the least, excessive, I became convinced that there were problems far less superficial. Overall, to characterize the staff as insensitive or intolerable of the young people enrolled in the program seemed unfair, even if *not always untrue*. Thus far, all of the sources discussed above give credence to the idea that colorblindness may be a basis for *mass intolerance* of black teenagers such as those in CSC and those living in South Carolina in general. Unlike micro-aggression, a term that assumes some association with accountability *and* identity, colorblindness does not. Colorblindness says "no" to acknowledging the impact of marginalization and young people, and "yes" to character assaults. This leaves little room for acknowledging the root of differentials in educational achievement and correctional practice –differentials that nearly always inscribe a race.

In his 2012 book "The Race for Class: Reflections on a Critical Raceclass Theory of Education," Zeus Leonardo notes that there are theorists that view CRT as a critical apparatus situating

---

10 Zeus Leonardo, 2012, p. 431

education (always) as a "racial project" - a key consideration in discussions about the staff/constituent relationship. Construct, SC fits best into an educational framework, as opposed to a job preparedness model. The program is not classroom-confined and provides a great deal of latitude in terms of enrollees' attendance, choice of educational track (a GED is not required to successfully complete the program) and other factors. In other words, we can logically discuss CSC in a combined *educational* and *CRT* context. Leonard notes that many education CRT scholars believe that there is no way of separating race and education. Those CRT theorists argue "that race and racism permeate the entire educational enterprise, from aspirations (Yosso 2006), to spatial configurations (Allen 1999), and teacher education itself" (Leonardo, 2012, p. 428). The permeation of race and education is observable at the center, but the complexity with which it pervades today is unexplored.

Up until the 1970s, White adolescent children were treated as valuable resources of the state and categorized as human capital. Certainly, White children may have been considered inputs and exploited for farm labor, but - at least according to the records – the activities were used in ensuring their adequate care and upkeep of the school. Included in the most basic care were formal education and the opportunity to learn trades because the expectation, it seems, is that the White children would soon reenter society and these skills would be of use to them. There were no formal educational opportunities at the RFB, nor does the institution seem to have been intent on teaching trades. In sum, we can conclude that sixty-plus years were invested in generations of White youth with the expectation of developing them, and so, perhaps to decrease the likelihood of delinquent behavior in the future.

For at *least 70 years*, Black adolescents were denied resources by the state and leveraged as inputs to support the state's correctional enterprise. Their able bodies were deployed in agricultural production, which minimized trade-oriented training opportunities. Therefore, if and when they were released, they would have been unprepared for industrial work or most other opportunities on par with boys from the industrial school. Black adolescents were governed by the state but not as children, but owned as criminals under South Carolina's penitentiary system and treated as such. There is no way of knowing whether the practices so clearly remarked upon in state reports subsided in ways that would have left the children with aspirations for the future; parole was not a possibility for at least the first twenty years of its operations. The spatial configurations were guarded by overseers and described as substandard. The boys were subject to transiency and commonly shipped to prison farms to work alongside adults.

The stark difference in the treatment of children, as described above, is framed in black and white terms. The *White-Black racial binary* that exists began with slavery, but continued in early divisions as those documented in early juvenile reform practice. A more common example is public school segregation until the late 1950s, which remained the binary far after South Carolina schools were integrated. There are class implications to this binary as well, as South Carolina's White Southerners moved unconstrained in the labor, education and social spheres, as mentioned. Although Black Southerners did enter industry and professional spheres such as education, they were highly restricted by racial boundaries, traditions and animus. This in turn resulted in Blacks staying within the structural confines, which encapsulated them. That is why the White–Black binary, at least in South Carolina, remains the dominant framework for understanding race and thus one of the few ways this study can deconstruct inter-generational deficits exhibited in the statistical reality of school removal and incarceration. Repeated cycles of blatant human rights violations against Black South Carolinians from enslavement to about the 1970s are one way of explaining the disproportionate statistical data provided earlier in this paper for context. Advancing these arguments as a means of causality is subject to much criticism, especially in a generation that may take comfort in fancying itself as *colorblind.*

Race is not black and white by definition, or in the diverse scope of an increasingly multiracial US and world. However, our understanding of *racism* is often framed as black and white; in South Carolina, this is not an oversimplification. On the other hand, racism is trivialized, often through microaggression as is later understood through the experiences of a SC news reporter noted in a later section of the paper. For now, I offer an example from the Community Center: I noticed that Black youths often wear his (or her) pants very low on the waist, something that often arouses suspicions by authority figure(s). This suspicion can be expressed in the form of critical questions like, *weren't you told not to sag*[11]*?* This is not only meant to vocalize disapproval, but often to make the young person aware of what the fashion statement implies *out there,* because they are vulnerable to public judgment. Community Center employees are sensitive about suspicions that may come from cultural outsiders and know these judgments will get in the way of potential work opportunities. I might also mention that African American employers are just as likely to misunderstand the fashion trend, yet less likely to rebuff a young person because of it, thus they are cultural insiders. The implication of so-called 'sagging' is in many respects an important dialogue and it does not seem irresponsible or cruel to make young people aware of the fact. There is, however, more critique of young people's attire than there is any coordinated effort to discuss with them *what the attire implies, to whom it implies it,* and reasons *why he or she may not know,* or *may not care to know,* how and why the discussion (or criticism) is relevant to them. This also goes back to a previous point made about colorblindness as a discussion blocker. Colorblindness deflects meaningful dialogue between youth and the trusted authority within the Center's organizational and racial sphere of understanding who can remind them of this simple point: sagging is a correctional fashion statement, at best and at worst, it can harm or kill. Any discussion about a young person's attire should be approached with

---

11 *Sag* is a term to describe youth and adults who wear pants very low on their waist and sometimes right below the buttocks. This trend developed in penitentiaries because belts can be used as weapons, thus when removed can result in sagging correctional attire.

compassion, considering it is one that mimics the real-world correctional landscape in which many Black boys and men loosely are born and reared. The colorblind point of view: then it is Black males who have created the correctional fashion culture and not the long history of disproportionate incarceration of Black prisoners itself. Most would agree that young people would benefit more from rational discussion than incessant pestering about the issue.

Critical Race Theory emancipates research like this from falsehoods of colorblindness, like those attempts to rationalize the murder of a 17 year-old Florida teenager named Trayvon Martin. Blogger-advocate Syretta McFadden's response to the not-guilty verdict for Martin's shooter was captured in this statement: *only in America can a dead black boy go on trial for his own murder*[12]. CRT affirms that if you are male, Black and living in the Southern United States, you can be accused, pursued or confronted if someone sees you and is intimidated by your attire, or so unnerved that they become afraid for their life and attempt to hurt you. CRT affirms that this person is likely to be White and male. On the other hand, colorblind-narrative upholds a far more neutral argument and does not give credence to viewpoints like McFadden's or the frustrations of authority such as those described at the Community Center.

---

12 Syreeta McFadden's statement on the verdict was shared the same statement on Facebook and was widely quote on many social media sites, Rabble.ca is a site containing blogs of Canadian "insightful, progressive activities and commenters ," is one: http://rabble.ca/blogs/bloggers/krystalline-kraus/2013/07/trayvon-martins-killer-walks-free

A final point about the colorblind perspective is that it often rejects histories, patterns, and trends that explain causation and often involve structural violence and inequality. Many of the sources used to show correctional and delinquent reform culture are premised on South Carolina's historic and well-documented practice of controlling enslaved Africans and their descendants. The research does not, however, intend to explain individual agency exercised by every Black adolescent having made decisions that result in school removal, juvenile or adult incarceration today. The research forwards the *relevancy* of the history with the expectation that it may one day be used to formulate solutions by scholars that might also believe in its relevancy.

The Problem

South Carolina's correctional culture is apparent in most arenas and organizational bodies, from the public school system to private non-profit organizations to municipal bodies in Sumter County. This corrections-laden culture was underscored earlier in the spring when I facilitated a presentation for teenagers seeking to obtain job skills at the Community Center. The program was aimed at teens partaking in a work program that would provide their first on-the-job training experience. The human resource director of the host organization agreed to speak with the teens to prepare them for the upcoming experience. She mainly discussed basic employment rules, organizational norms, breaks, etc. Near the end, I asked the group of teenagers if they had any questions for the director. They all said nothing; some shook their head to indicate *no*. After a long silence, I asked the director to discuss a few basic rules or norms of the workplace (e.g., cell phone *use* and other forms of office etiquette). She proceeded to warn against using inappropriate language and cell phones during work time. In hopes of establishing protocols that the teens could identify should they make a misstep, I asked how the young people would be warned regarding rule breaking. She responded that the "first offense" would likely yield a warning, but "repeat offenders" would incur more serious consequences and that "good behavior" would always be taken into consideration. Several days later I had the opportunity to ask that group of teens whether the presentation was helpful. I waited for answers, but many moments of silence passed. I encouraged them to speak up, as the discussion was relevant in preparing them for an upcoming work experience. One young man started to speak up, but was interrupted by another who raised his hand and started speaking simultaneously: "I don't know... I am sure (pause)...I mean, no offense, but she seemed kind of mean-like," (Community Center Teen, private communication, May, 2014). The young man that was interrupted simply affirmed the first teen's statement with, "Yeah..." after which, a few other teens nodded in agreement (Community Center Teen 2, private communication, May, 2014). To calm any nerves, I told them that my few experiences with the director were friendly, and that there was no reason to think their experience with her would be any different. I was compelled to ask if they had heard the correctional terms as I did. The answer was *yes.* Many nodded; some clearly said "yes", and recalled some words I had not heard or simply forgotten. I was convinced the hush that came over the customarily lively group of teenagers muted them. In Sumter County, one might say their voices were detained and the group dynamics that I observed consistently as lively were cuffed in the 30-minute presentation.

What was so mean-like about her? I could not correlate a race or age bias because the director is black and is likely in her mid-to-late 30s. She was dressed very nicely, but not to a level that would isolate her audience. She did not speak over or under the group of teens and I feel she explained her points well. If she were in a school, she may have been mistaken for an administrator or teacher;

however, the manner in which she made her points was likely the reason for the students to disengage. The explanations she provided were logical, but carried a serious tone that might have conveyed to the group that their upcoming work experience would be too rigorous to enjoy. I heard the correctional terms at the end, but according to the teens, there were a few used beforehand. If this was the case, it did not seem to help in gaining or building the confidence of the young people. In all fairness, this was not the objective of her talk that day, but rather a nuance that offers insight into how young people characterize authority (like employers or teachers) based on how they are spoken to.

This anecdote is intended to show how an ordinary presentation, perhaps lackluster at worst, aroused perceptions of *meanness*. The wrong perception of a young person can disengage them and thus leave an impression that the authority figure is uncaring or perhaps unapproachable. There are many young people, not only Construct, SC program participants that attend alternative educational courses at the Community Center because of a situation that left them with similar perceptions of adults. In casual dialogue with young people at the Center, they often recited experiences of being removed from school, such as the following:

I was kicked out because of (blank). The (authority) said I did (blank) or said (blank). That is actually what happened... The (authority) only saw/heard (blank), but I didn't do/say (blank). The specific (authority) always wrote me up or referred me in order to

get me in trouble. [The authority] says, I can't go back - or - I can't
go back until next school year.

Perceptions are *perceptions* for a reason, and this study does
not forward the discussion above as to suggest it as *observation.*
Rather, this pseudo-dialogue is one that, first, connects to *my*
observation of how sensitive the teens were to the speaker's
presentation. Let us recall, the presenter did nothing overtly
threatening or intentional to intimidate the teens. It is likely that the
teenagers interpreted the speaker as *mean-like* because of the
authoritative manner in which she explained the rules and guidelines
of a new experience. None of the teenagers had work experience; to
hear the director discuss rules and enforcement on the work site may
have added to their nervousness.

State Authority in Education and Corrections

At this juncture in the paper, we turn to more recent statistics
that offer information that may substantiate arguments stated earlier
in the paper. As a recap of what has been covered and the objectives
thus far, the study's effort to hear from Black adults that were not
long ago considered adolescents by the state is the primary objective,
and to provide context for explaining their experiences. It occurred
to me that experiences were often shared, but perhaps not closely
examined as to alert the efficacy in understanding, at this present
time, what Black adolescents are facing in Sumter County and
elsewhere across the country. In this study's *Review of the Literature*
I intended to provide information to ground the reader in

understanding the immense powers exercised by the state of South Carolina - not only during slavery, but also thereafter in a concerted effort, specifically, against Black males to exploit their labor and quite possibly reinstitute control through criminalization, as was present during the period of enslavement.

Separation of Races in Public Schools: Then And Now

South Carolina's public school systems remain challenged by racism and segregation. To show how race permeates schools today, I offer a local case known by many in Sumter County and the surrounding community simply as *"Briggs."*

Briggs versus Elliot. Summerton, South Carolina, is home to the appeals case originating in Clarendon County. *Briggs versus. Elliot* was the first of five cases chosen and combined into what became *Brown versus Board of Education*. As a result, the United States Supreme Court determined that racial segregation is unconstitutional.

In a 2011 news story by *The Sumter Item*, honoring Summerton's historic role, the headline read "Briggs v. Elliott: Summerton schools still mostly segregated" (Baker, 2011). The article served to commemorate, but also examine the 2011 landscape that appeared to remain largely segregated. Leola Parks was one of 13 Black students that first integrated Summerton High school. Parks graduated in 1970 and now works for Clarendon County (SC) District 1. Upon reflection, Park recalled, "You know, we kept to ourselves, and the white students, they kept to themselves," she said.

"We continued to do our own things. And then, most of the white students left the school and it closed," (Baker, 2011). Unfortunately, students were unable to unify. This was not only the result of Black youth entering the local high school, but White teens migrating out and some by executive order, as reported: "[White students] crossed district lines to Clarendon District 2, through an oral executive order handed down from a state judge allowing White students to transfer to neighboring districts," (Baker, 2011).

Rose Wilder, who grew up minutes away from Summerton, is now Clarendon County 1 Superintendent. She was also interviewed in the article and remarked that a "difficult part in Clarendon 1 [school district] is that we've had two totally different communities. I just wish that we could bring those together to utilize the talent we have in these communities," (Baker, 2011).

Alternatively, the headmaster of Clarendon Hall, a private k-12 school, Kimberly Fleming, cited desegregation as *'a part'* of the school's founding. Fleming is no longer headmaster of the school, but commented in the 2011 story that the influx of white students to Clarendon Hall was also a response to secular attitudes forming at the time. Fleming said, "Many private schools around that time were formed for those same reasons," (Baker, 2011).

Criminal Stereotyping of Black Males in South Carolina: Now and Then

> "Like I don't like how they talk about it like that. I'd like to hear a black person talk about it cause they sound more hurt about it. Like White people talk they sound like they got a lot of encouragement like 'Yeah, we did that, like they can't run over us type junk' and they scared to death of you and they see a black person walking pass they car or something and they be locking they door, acting like they on their phone talking to somebody" (Interviewee, private communication, 2014).

This is one Construct, SC enrollee's remark upon reflection on his least favorite subject, *Social Studies*. When I asked him why he felt this way about this particular subject he answered with the statement above. From what we can gather from his statement, having to sit in a classroom and listen to histories relating to African Americans was unpleasant. But hearing the history from a person that he perceived as being insensitive to the history, made the experience even more unpleasant. From the interviewee's experience, we can surmise that at least one of his White teachers has treated African American history with some callousness. He then says, White people are 'scared to death' of Black people, which I interpret as a tongue-in-cheek way of asserting that given the history, it should be the other way around. This is open to interpretation, but clearly the interviewee connects social studies and race history as being one reason why bias and stereotypes exist today. If indeed the person in a vehicle the interviewee reflects upon locked his or her door because they saw him approaching, then this would be criminal stereotyping.

Stereotyping is Prevalent in SC Today

During and after the Trayvon Martin case, personal narratives emerged from unlikely places, namely news journalists. Warren Bolton, a South Carolina Associate Editor for *The State* who writes primarily about local politics and government, but who also delves at times into social commentary, like so many other journalists, was compelled to offer his thoughts on the case. What he offers about his own experiences as a native of Columbia, the state capital, is far more interesting and pertinent to this study then commentary about Martin. For example:

> While in college, a white female editor told me she didn't think we were going to get along. It was her first time meeting me, along with the other dozen or so interns. The internship was with a North Carolina newspaper; I wasn't the only one from Columbia or South Carolina or the South. I wasn't the only male. But I was the only African-American. Bolton offers personal micro-aggressive situations in which he found himself growing up in South Carolina, and states that his "Examples might seem trivial to some people. But no one wants to spend a lifetime under suspicion. No one should have to" (Bolton, 2013).

The statement is followed by an example of his most important experience yet, fatherhood. Bolton is the father of two boys, who he states in the story as being four and eight years old. As most Black fathers asserted after the profiling and killing of Trayvon Martin, he explains to his readership that it is *critical* that he prepare his sons for the day they will be "picked up, called *that* name, accused of *that* transgression. We just don't know when" (Bolton 2013). He ends his commentary by pointing out an incident that occurred with children at a South Carolina summer camp:

> Recently, my younger son accompanied me to drop his big brother off at camp. When I stepped up to sign my son in, a white female staffer referred to them both — they are ages 4 and 8 — as my "criminal children." Very bad joke? Stupid? Dumb? Bad judgment? Racist? She said it twice; the words easily rolled off her tongue. Infuriated, I called her on it — and not so kindly, I must confess — and she apologized. But what was I to tell my 4-year-old, who kept asking: "Who is she talking about, daddy?" The two little black boys at my side (Bolton, 2013).

George Stinney Jr. - The "Bully"[13]

To date, South Carolina holds the record for executing the youngest person in the United States in the last century (view Appendix 8: George Stinney Jr. of Alcolu, SC). In an article published in June of this year, a New York Times reporter, Jesse Wegman, describes 14 year-old George Stinney's death by

---

[13] "Bully" is how a living relative of the two young victims Binnicker and Thames referred to Stinney in a 2014 NBC News story.
Link:http://www.nbcnews.com/news/investigations/victims-niece-argues-against-retrial-1944-murder-case-n14651

electrocution as a "lynching in slow motion" but a *legal* one nonetheless (Wegman, 2014). In the opinion pages Wegman opines, "The sentencing report states that George Stinney was "legally" electrocuted, however, to describe what happened to Stinney as legal is to say "only that this boy's fate was decided in a courtroom by a judge and jury, rather than by a throng of angry men with a rope" (2014). Frankly, it *was* a legal execution and it was based on evidence that Stinney family attorneys (active today) contend was highly unlikely to have been committed by Stinney. The two young victims, Betty June Binnicker and Mary Emma Thames, were "found beaten to death in a ditch in rural Clarendon County, SC" (Wegner, 2014). Recently, a South Carolinian by the name of Wilford Hunter issued an official statement given the possibility a Stinney retrial. According to Hunter, he shared a cell with Stinney for only a few days, but recalls Stinney telling him, 'I didn't do it' and 'why would they kill me for something I didn't do?' (2014). The question is haunting for the generations after Stinney. Stinney's parents were not included in his *confession*[14] and were otherwise run out of Alcolu, South Carolina, upon mob threats (NBC News, 2014).

Corrections Today

According to The Sentencing Project, if you are male and black the likelihood of you spending a part of your life imprisoned is 1 in 3 (The Sentencing Project [TSP], 2014). The truth is, ever since correctional institutions emerged, at least in the South, show that

Black males as more representative in jails than White counterparts. I have yet to come across a statistic that shows otherwise. South Carolina's first correctional facilities were established in 1866, granting control of convicted felons from counties to the state (SCDOC, 2014). Over time, it has developed a reputation for operating penitentiaries that are not only state of the art but efficient – so much so that an Iraqi delegation made a two-week visit with a U.S. Justice official and 'counterparts' to gain understanding of its operations and gather information they could apply in their country (Kinnard, 2007).

In 2013, The PEW Charitable Trust (PEW) condensed compiled a brief history of South Carolina's growing incarceration rates over the last 30 years:

> Over the past 25 years, South Carolina's prison population has soared from 9,137 inmates in 1983, to 24,612 at the end of 2009—and was projected to grow by more than 3,200 inmates by 2014. This growth has come at a significant cost to South Carolina's taxpayers. In 1983, the state spent $63.7 million on prison operations. By 2008, correctional expenditures had skyrocketed to $394.1 million. (2013).

By 2009, the rising and projected costs of incarcerating mostly petty criminals were enough for then-Governor Mark Sanford to sign legislation to reform the practice. A joint statement from former U.S. House Speaker Newt Gingrich and Prison Fellowship Vice President Pat Nolan said this in support of the reform:

About half of South Carolina's prison population is being held for nonviolent offenses... Such low-level violations, as well as certain nonviolent drug-related crimes, can be punished in other ways that aren't as expensive as prison. We build prisons for people we're afraid of. Yet South Carolina has filled them with people we're just mad at" (Right on Crime [ROC], 2010).

As expenditures increased, South Carolina addressed rising incarceration rates in 2010 with a cost-saving act that projected savings estimated at $241 million (ROC, 2010). Addressing the state's incarceration numbers meant also addressing *why* so many people were behind bars. In 2013, the SCDOC reported that out of 20,777 male prisoners, 13, 631 were Black. Based on the findings reported in 2010, many of those are locked up for petty crime (e.g., personal possession of marijuana). As well as being known for locking up petty offenders, South Carolina is also known for holding the number one position in the nation for domestic killing of women by men (Phillips, 2013).

Criminal Terminology

Language seems to play an integral role in how young people feel about authority and the manner in which they assert themselves. In an effort to legitimize my observation of teenagers' negative reactions to correctional language, I engaged a friend[15] to share her expertise. Her experience in education and mental health is

---

[15] Anonymous source

extensive. She has taught at more than three South Carolina schools over the course of seven years, leading courses designed for different age classes (e.g., elementary, middle and high school). Additionally, she maintains a contracted partnership with a mental health facility and is familiar with protocols at large mental health facilities.

I sent an e-mail asking for a statement that might substantiate my observation of how prevalent criminal language is in schools and the workplace, at least in Sumter County. I asked if she could substantiate the language in the counseling policy and procedures of her work site (a mental health facility) and at the schools where she has taught. Her reply:

> Yes. Even in schools we use words like *put the kids on lockdown*. This affects Black children because the majority of them had or has a family member in the penal system. We also use things like code of conduct and *level offenses*. As far as the [mental health facility] over the years we changed the culture to the engagement model where we take into account the fact that someone has had some trauma in his or her life. Our number one job is to talk them through it. Before that time we used words like *lockdown*, *lights out*, and *takedown* (M.B. personal communication, June 3, 2014).

She further explains in a second reply that, often, African American educators tend to demonstrate more sensitivity and omit the language when speaking to children:

> They [African American staff] are more sensitive to the students in regard to this type of language. This was not the

case at another school I worked and African-Americans were in the minority across the board. They were exposed to a lot of the criminal type language (M.B., personal communication, June 3, 2014).

There are many conversations resulting from my participant observation that left me jarred. I often heard the phrases "I just never went back" or "I was told I can't come back" and "I needed to try next year." In the case of Construct, SC, I repeatedly heard staff remark that an enrollee was not *serious* and that *someone else could take his or her place... someone that really deserves it.* I also observed staff sequestering the personal property of enrollees and locking it up in a portable safe that was only reopened on breaks. This was not used to secure the personal or valuable possessions of the students, but as a way of enforcing a *no cell phone policy* during instructional periods. In the least, I found the formality highly inappropriate in the treatment of young *adults.* The program is designed to build confidence and accountability, so such a formality seemed to counter these efforts; instead, they were empty gestures of obedience enrollees should have been asked to exhibit. The final point (and most perplexing) is that the staff rarely adhered to policies regarding *their* cell phones, which I saw to be dismissed despite reminders from the Director. Staff would repeatedly bring cell phones to meetings, scroll through information during instructional periods, and even play games when disinterested during meetings. Thus, hypocrisy has been a hindrance in establishing positive staff/constituent relationship. My view was the CSC participants could never understand and practice responsible cell phone usage if the adults responsible for setting the example chose not to.

There is also a lot scrutiny about constituent attire, which can be ill fitted or represent correctional attire. The locking up of cell phones and scrutiny about attire can make a distrusting or uncomfortable environment. In "Counterspaces: A Unit of Analysis for Understanding the Role of Settings in Marginalized Individuals' Adaptive Responses to Oppression," Andrew D. Case and Carla D. Hunter theorize that individual wellbeing can improve amongst groups that have experienced marginalization or oppression. They address a number of *adaptive responses* to do this, but narrative is considered key.

Recall that the study began because my observations of the CSC class were starkly different in comparison to the experiences of the staff. I heard snippets about their lives, sometimes in ways I found to be highly insensitive and dismissive to the gravity of what those experiences would mean to other people: *he's homeless, he saw his mother murdered, he's hungry, he's an alcoholic, he smokes [marijuana], he's not serious, he probably won't pass, he's in a gang, he doesn't come, he's unappreciative, he's not a leader, he needs to cut his hair, he needs to pull up his pants, he needs to apologize, etc.* So it seemed appropriate to hear from them first-hand, if they wanted to share their stories, to understand how these labels developed in micro setting (Sumter County). Case and Hunter (2012) summarize the narrative identifying work as a re-crafting of self-concepts, which they explain in the following excerpt:

Counterspace members draw on setting-level narratives[16] as well as identity-affirming experiences within counterspaces to re-craft self-concepts that have been "devastated by the larger culture…personal narratives are re-imagined within counterspaces out of necessity due to meta-communications of *otherness* and *inferiority* transmitted through negative dominant cultural narratives and specific experiences of oppression. These negative dominant cultural narratives are most easily identified as pejorative stereotypes. African Americans, for example, are thought of as being lazy, boisterous, angry, criminal and unintelligent (Deaux et al. 2007; Jones 1997). (p. 261).

Case and Hunter's critical approach offers insights that are integral in advancing many of the positions contained in this paper. More so, they offer realistic approaches that do not shrug off oppression, but rather acknowledge its impact even on generations far removed from its more blatant forms. In South Carolina, resistance by young Black youth to being marginalized by other racial groups is thought to be unhelpful to them – or at least this was the opinion of one CSC teacher. He told me about a former CSC student of his that quit a job on his 'first day' because an older White man, a 'Jew' called him 'Boy' and he 'didn't like that," (CSC

---

16 In essence, the enhancement of one's sense of self in the face of oppression can and often is facilitated through the presence of strategic others (Case and Hunter, 2012, p.261).

Teacher, private communication, May 2014). Clearly, the White middle-age teacher, also from Sumter County, understood the implications because he volunteered the story. I did not want to disengage the teacher by asking *if he did* understand the implications, so I decided to move on to better understand his view on the matter. The teacher was certain that *another young man would have picked that job up in a minute.* I might also mention that this teacher is well respected by the students and is one of the most prepared of all the CSC staff that I observed.

In some ways the young man in the teacher's story rejected the term, or the microaggression, one could say. Whether or not the employer understood the weight of the term cannot accurately be judged. There could have been no harm intended, but from the perspective of the young man, it was at least upsetting enough to walk off a job that he likely wanted and needed. However, I make this point because the colorblind perspective makes a relevant history *irrelevant,* even in the case of young former CSC enrollee that rejected a term he knew and understand to be a racial diminutive.

Generations of Africans and their descendants in South Carolina were oppressed under chattel slavery, then again during the Reconstruction Era, and up until the 1960s in correctional facilities. The question then: where does colorblindness, racial and correctional terminology, fit in the lives of CSC constituents? Case and Hunter's 'Counterspace' framework proposes a theory applicable to Black youth who live with the tradition and practices of

South Carolina's exploitative reform praxis. The injury that Case and Hunter perceive is of the critical theoretical perspective and is best explained by the excerpt below:

> We argue that Counterspaces can be thought of as settings, which promote positive self-concepts among marginalized individuals (e.g., racial and sexual minority individuals, persons with disabilities, etc.) through the challenging of deficit-oriented dominant cultural narratives and representations concerning these individuals (p. 261).

'Counterspaces' are essentially settings and, according to the authors', if facilitated correctly can aid in healing injured groups overcoming negative stereotypes. On the other hand, *adaptive responding* is described as a transactional process by which marginalized individuals seek to maintain psychological wellness in the face of oppression (Case & Hunter, 2012).

Essentially, counterspaces can be organizations, systems of support and range from informal to formal (p. 262). The authors discuss oppression and marginalization effectually, meaning, the argument is that there are ways of challenging negative climates to bring about 'healing' and 'restoration'. Case and Hunter (2012) identify three general domains of "challenging processes likely to be present in most counterspaces" to be *narrative work, acts of resistance*, and *direct relational transactions* (view Appendix 13: Case and Hunter).

Portraits

My interview respondents gave me permission to document their cases and make scholarly presentations of my findings to an audience of my peers. Respondent names and sensitive information have been modified in order to avoid offering specifics that could reveal their identities. For example, instead of specifying the name of the public school a respondent attended, I classify the institution as "High School A" or "High School B" located in a "Neighboring County" or "County."

The line of questioning typically began with basic biographical information. In most cases, this allowed the narrative provided by interviewees to build chronologically depending on how they chose to elaborate on their individual experience. The males' experiences in the public school system were helpful in retrieving how they view their personal characteristics, critical moments, and thought processes amid situations and circumstance.

Mitchell

Mitchell is over eighteen years of age and describes himself as 'quiet' and especially good in mathematics. He was born in Sumter County and grew up in a small inner city located within it. In describing his early elementary school experiences, Mitchell notes that he was not always a quiet person. His earliest school memories are of being the "class clown" and telling jokes that would make both children and teachers laugh. He shared his thoughts on what elementary school means to a young child. He offers that elementary school is very important in early childhood development and admits to being 'bad' when he was young: " I was bad (laughs). Bad and adventurous. You start to develop more learning skills in elementary school…. That's your start, that's where you start right there. Meeting people, talking to teachers…it was fun though." (Mitchell, personal communication, May 2014). He also stated that there was not much he didn't like about elementary school, except getting 'written up.' As a young elementary student, he remembers some of his ruckus to include drawing on clothes and 'other' people's things, or shouting 'little' jokes in class (2014). When asked later if he could provide an example of a specific prank he pulled or something that was especially humorous or significant, he replies:

> The only thing I remember is my homeboy had some gum one day…I said 'Man can I get a piece of gum?' Him and me were friends, or associates – actually we're like brothers. We at school. We tussling over the piece of gum. I swear we went to class [after tussling] and all. Next thing I know, we hear our names come into the office. We're like 'Why are we being called?' Come to know, a teacher on the low seen us and wrote us up and didn't even tell us. She waited until we got good in class doing our work too. We're in two different classrooms now. He's across the hall so when they called our name, we both open the door like 'What in the world! We were just playing over gum! What in the world would I fight my homeboy over a piece of gum for?" Once we're in the

office, the principal's office, he can't do anything but laugh about it. [The principal said] 'You must have really wanted that gum, cause here you are chewing it.' I said to myself 'Oh, look at these people here.' The principal tore the referrals up and told me 'Go back to class.' I say, 'I know that teacher was a mean teacher.' She wrote up, didn't tell the principal and us said we were written up for nothing... we weren't fightin, we were just playin. (Mitchell, 2014).

This was a significant moment because around eight years of age, Mitchell sums up this experience as one in which he learned that he could "not to play like that no more" (2014). By the end of fifth grade, he began skipping school, as he says to 'pick pecans.'

The skipping school and pecan picking continued. Mitchell adds that, although he received a regular allowance from a parent or grandparent, nothing could replace the money he could earn by pecan picking for a few hours a day: as much as $200-$300 on a good day. He does not consider the labor that generated this income to be traditional work, as he states, "I never ever had a job" (Mitchell, 2014). He quickly adds that he is not sure why and says, "I guess I was always in school; getting kicked in and out of school. I never really thought about being at no new job like that" (Mitchell, 2014).

When Mitchell says that he has 'never' had a job, it seems to me he has and, although informal, it counts. Mitchell's picking and selling pecans provided him income and allowed him to exercise economic agency. After he shares the earning potential of a day pecan picking, he also states that he 'bought shoes' and didn't 'save' which is, as I understand it, with some regret.

On the other hand, Mitchell is certain about many decisions and circumstances regarding his life. He quotes his late grandmother's adages frequently and then describes how he rationalized it in his life at the time:

> [Heeding her advice] She said you didn't have to worry about getting in trouble, getting locked up, none of that, nothing stupid. In the store stealing, she didn't like that or a liar and a thief. She didn't like that, my grandma. She said, 'Boy don't you ever be a liar or a thief." She always used to say 'Boy, you'll lie before a cat can wink his eye' (laughs). She used to always tell me that (laughs) cause I did used to lie bad though. I had to break out of that habit. (2014)

Concerning his own friendships, Mitchell adopted his grandmother's perspective. She told him at one point that he had 'no friends' and not to bring 'hoodlums' to her house. He elaborates, saying the following:

> I don't believe in best friends, I don't too much believe in friends. My grandma told me not to. She told me 'Boy you ain't got friends, you ain't never gonna have friends.' I say 'Yes, ma'am, I already know that.' I am like that until this day now. They always go to backstab you. (2014)

His grandmother regularly sent him to rural country areas as punishment when she learned of his chronic tardiness; it was employed to 'tighten' him up, as Mitchell puts it. He explains that the older he became, the less he liked being sent to the country to stay with relatives. He was charged with *In-School Disturbance* at one local high school and almost 'caught CDV charge,' which is the abbreviation for *Criminal Domestic Violence.* This was the result of an incident that took place at school involving his ex-girlfriend. He admits to tripping the young woman as she attempted to walk away from an argument they were having. In a follow-up question at the end of our interview, I asked Mitchell if he could name a relationship(s) that he would like to repair. His first answer was the relationship with his grandmother, and the second relationship would be with the ex-girlfriend he tripped at school that day.

He never returned to high school after this specific incident and, at the time, preferred not to return. His expulsion did not involve a hearing, but rather the assumption that he would not return; he quickly remarks that as being the "crazy thing about it" (2014). The previous in-school clash happened at the very beginning of the school year when a gym teacher wrote him up for writing on his own clothes. The principal said that he did not understand why any student would pay $20-$30 of his or her own money to ruin school attire with graffiti. The principal dismissed the write-up or referral. Despite being understood by the principal, Mitchell ended up tossing his clothes in the trashcan out of frustration. He explains his perspective as follows:

> Gym teacher was like, *You're not going to kick him out?* I
> had to go through a hearing and all just because this teacher
> kept picking about the situation or whatever. I was really

close to gettin kicked out because of that gym teacher. She was trying her best to get me kicked out of [High School A]. (2014)

After asking follow-up questions, Mitchell discloses that the graffiti included gang symbols. This prompts another follow up question: *What do the symbols mean to you?* His answer:

People think they [gangs] are dangerous, you got [Group A][17] and [Group B][18] who all know each other in the same area. It's about money, as long as you getting money, you don't get disrespected or aren't disrespectful to another set [19]or whatever. Like, someone gets upset cause someone else is getting more money than ya'll —then you come together. That's how everyone starts to see it now. People are like 'Bump the colors.' It ain't about colors, cause you "Group A" and got [this color][20] on, I'm gonna shoot you. Or you "Group B" and got on [that color], I'm gonna shoot you. Naw, you get money we gonna leave all that beef[21] and problems alone. That is how it coming up now. (2014)

---

[17] "Group A" is a pseudonym for local gang historically opposed to "Group B"
[18] "Group B" is a pseudonym for local gang historically opposed to "Group A"
[19] "Set" a synonym for gang group or affiliation
[20] Colors are a way of identifying gangs, and are often popularized in pop culture references. The specific colors are omitted so not to directly associate "Mitchell" with any affiliation past or present.
[21] "Beef" is used here as a synonym for conflict

Donald

Donald is over eighteen years old and has lived in the state
most of his life. He was sent to live with a great-grandparent before
the age of three. He recalls traveling extensively over the north and
Southeastern United States in his childhood. However, his favorite
state is one he has yet to visit. *Really?* I ask. *Which state?* Around
the age of ten or eleven, he began considering Tennessee to be a
state with a strong community, and flourishing business
environment. Donald sees his future as a businessman and would
like to own establishments like restaurants, gas stations and maybe a
car dealership. He explains, "I came up from doing the wrong things
in life to doing the right things. People realizing. Just [to] be known
for something good," he laughs. "Yeah, I want to be seen" (Donald,
personal communication, May 2014). The notoriety he desires he
believes could help his business, so that he can help his community.
He describes his developing business acumen this way: "[Good]
attire, dressing right, do your work, if someone needs help, take time
out to help him. Don't waste too much time. Be respectful, loyal, and
get work done." (Donald, 2014)

I ask him what he finds most sacred, and in addition to his
first answer, "money" (laughs), he quickly adds "my grandmother's
house." I ask him to elaborate on what his grandmother's home
represents to him. He replies, "Things that have happened. Family.
Love. Situations. Mmm…basically life" (Donald, 2014). The two
answers (money and grandma's house) are related, it seems, by how
he describes her as a hardworking, independent retiree who "kept

up" and "paid" for her home. His grandmother was present in his life even in times of trouble and would send Donald to the country if he got out of line. In elementary school, he describes himself as "Quiet sometimes... Friendly" (2014).

In middle school Donald joined a football team and actively engaged in mathematics: his favorite subject. He describes how he changed from being 'quiet' to being more assertive in middle school. According to Donald, he knew with certainty that someone stole from him and when he confronted his peer at school, the peer simply answered he had not taken anything from him. Donald explains: "I tried to talk to this person about it and they act like they didn't know what was going on. So I got mad: got in his face" (2014). A physical altercation was avoided, but he was still suspended. He finishes recounting by stating that he felt "disrespected" by his peer for not telling him the truth, and obviously for stealing from him (Donald, 2014).

This situation made him "tone down for a little while" and focus on football and school. However, his referrals increased, as did the severity of his in-school offenses. By the end of the year, Donald was suspended again for showing shirttails[22]. In [Grade 7] "Suspended again. I think the first one was dress code, like something to do with my shirt, my shirttails. [I was] Fighting and hanging with the wrong people. Bad things" (Donald, 2014).

However, a more serious incident ensued when Donald was identified in an after-school group scuffle at the bus area. He says,

---

[22] *Shirttails* is a term used to describe an un-tucked shirt; considered sloppy.

"They found out who had been involved and they kicked us out. Expulsion. This was near the end, like March or February. They called everyone they could have named in the office. They said I had hit somebody. I went home, left the house. Started fighting in my neighborhoods" (Donald, 2014).

Donald describes the fights as serious at times. He shares an incident in which shortly after seeing his brother leave for school, a bullet was shot through the window of his residence, landing above his bed frame. When I ask Donald how many times he's been shot at, he said three altogether: the first one happened in the 'country' where his grandmother would send him to refocus. The 'country' is often how South Carolinians and perhaps many Southerners in general describe places that lie outside of larger city centers and essentially means a rural area. The third incident took place near his residence at the time, similar to the one he has just explained.

He eventually was re-enrolled in the same alternative school that had treated him and other students like "children", requiring they adhere to specific rules like "walking around the halls, instead of crossing, you have to walk all around" (Donald, 2014). One day, a teacher "flipped" on him because he neglected to follow the "walk around rule" when he stepped out of class to get a drink of water in the hallway. Up until this point, Donald describes the school as lacking "important stuff" he needed, like football and math. Donald was sent to jail for *In-School Disturbance*, ordered to attend and pay for anger management class, and was required to pay a $200 bond. This is how he describes the incident:

She [teacher] wasn't even in her classroom; she was worrying about the wrong people for one thing. I was just going to get some water and she just flipped out, so I just flipped out, too. At first, I didn't know I was going on cause I'd never been in their jail. I didn't know what we were supposed to be doing. I called people to get me out. (Donald, 2014)

The principal said Donald could attempt to re-enroll for the next school year. After finding himself out of school, Donald took on odd jobs around his neighborhood like cutting grass. By the time he reached High School A, he made no effort to join the team because of the strict grade, attendance, and drug testing requirements. He retained his math appreciation and abilities: math is a subject he refers to as "easy," with a smile. However, he collected referrals for *shirttails* and *sagging*. He says his last year attempt (in grade 11) at public school failed because "It just felt different, so I just stopped. Stopped going to school" (2014). He attempted to gain his GED at a local Adult Education Program, but said he was never given the test because his practice tests were too low. He explains, "I was going there for so long; walking up there back and forth" (2014). In fact, Donald specifies he was going there for over a year when he finally took the advice of a friend that suggested Construct, SC. Donald obtained his GED in 2013 through the Construct, SC program.

One of the last questions I ask Donald is: *what is something you would like people to know about you that they may not know already?* He responds: "I still have work to do. I am starting something new; I ain't never done in my life. New beginnings, it's great. It's good, it's good… I'd like the world to know I am a successful grown man with a lot of potential. With my own thing and a lot of money [to earn]. That I can help others, if they need help or want help" (2014).

Troy

It was Jamon that encouraged Troy to consider Construct, SC. He tells me that they met at a shelter located in the local area, recalling that "He [Jamon] said he was getting his 'life together' and that it could help me get my life together" (Troy, personal communication, May 2014). Troy tells me that his life growing up was "structured" and that he was provided for (2014). He feels that not having his education limits him in ways so that he "can't go nowhere and can't do nothing" (Troy, 2014). He considers this time in the Community Center as one that requires him to focus and pay attention or "observe" opportunities. He speaks of the difference between urban life and suburban life and ultimately believes that people in urban dwellings will strive harder for their education than those living in suburbia. He offers this observation of other young adults that began the program with him:

> It's more of the initiative. In low poverty neighborhoods, like the ones that come here [resource center] it's a little wacky and tacky right now cause the staff and everything going on, but at the middle of mental toughness you'll see that everybody can be cordial and punctual; they can be on time.

During orientation, nobody missed a day. They were there eight o'clock on the dot. They dressed up to show they can and wanted to be here... I don't think you'd see any kids in the 'sub' area do that, or even dress up" (2014).

Troy suggests that the image of freedom in the United States is open to interpretation depending on one's cultural lens. He recalls meeting international students that assumed he listened to a lot of rap music or maybe exclusively rap music. He claims that even though he moved to South Carolina from another southern state, it was a culture shock and that he did not do his "research," which relates to the trouble he found himself in and recounts soon after. He explains: "South Carolina laws are stricter than the other state and I did not know that - didn't do my research before I moved here. Didn't know nothin about nothin, which is why I had to go through a lot of court problems, and dealing with them" (Troy, 2014).

Troy says his father tried to shelter him and give him good advice that makes sense now. He says that he listened to his father's attempt to "teach me about life" and that while he was very young and did not understand, he was "listening though" (Troy, 2014). He often thinks of his father's advice when he has to "catch himself" feeling down or overwhelmed by his responsibilities (2014). He explains, "If I get over bombarded with a lot of responsibilities... I get wrapped up in my own mind then I just shut down completely" (Troy, 2014). He recalls a moment when I saw him sitting alone in a classroom at the Community Center and tells me why he was sad that day.

She [CSC teacher] had pulled me to the side earlier and said: 'Look I am going to have to send you to another educational center if you don't start coming like you're supposed to because someone else can take your spot and that it seems to me you really don't want it' …and she kind of hurt me a little bit. I do want to be in the program. (Troy, 2014).

I acknowledge that I remember that day, but also mentioned that when I offered to listen, he preferred not share with me at that time. He explains now that it was the CSC teacher that upset him and was thus the cause of his being "down" (Troy, 2014). He was hurt by the instructor's comments because he had missed those particular days to handle some legal business. *I did not want to be intrusive,* I say. He responds, "I had been triggered, not by you [interviewer], but with me dealing with this teacher. I know what I've been doing since I've been done with all my court problems" (Troy, 2014). He offers, as his last comment on the topic, that "If that was the case [not wanting to show up], I wouldn't bother coming the days I do come and dealing with my little problems" (Troy, 2014).

We discuss his relocation to South Carolina, which Troy describes as life changing. He was in school for a few months, noting he hadn't developed a real sense for the school when he says, "an in-school informant caught me" (Troy, 2014). He recalls the experience as "surreal" and one involving a South Carolina Sheriff who enlisted school districts in his jurisdiction to "test" sting operations. Troy describes the circumstances leading to his arrest on two serious charges as being *"curious"*: a situation involving another

59

young man who he thought was becoming a very good friend. Troy explains that he received a text from his former friend stating that a peer of theirs wanted to purchase some marijuana. Troy elaborates:

> Told him to go ahead and handle it [complete sale] 'cause we were doing it that way. Basically, I was putting him in with me to get a little bit of money; too…He was the popular one in school. He wasn't an investigator; I guess he'd gone through some kind of court trouble himself. How we got caught - I go give him a handshake, a solid handshake, he's supposed to slide out of my hand like usual. I go my way, he goes his way. He [unexpectedly] turned around and dropped it. As I am walking away from the cafeteria door and he's walking towards the cafeteria door. An administrator was looking through the window the whole time. The administrator pages the cop and says to me 'Hey, you! You! Stop right there. Now come back this way and pick up that thing with you' (Troy, 2014).

Troy believes there are only two ways a scenario like this happens: either there is a confidential informant sent by police, or those offering to set up someone else to get themselves out of trouble. He maintains that the young man's name was never mentioned in his court proceedings, nor was it ever listed in any court documents he reviewed. He adds, "On top of that, when it was brought up in court, *he* [former friend] wasn't brought up. He's still going to school, [as though] everything is fine" (Troy, 2014). Matters escalated when police learned he had a vehicle in which they found a pistol, thus resulting in two charges relating to the distribution of marijuana and the illegal possession of a firearm. I inquire about the purpose of having the gun, and he states "protection," and that "anyone selling anything should have something." Troy was told to have an adult come to the school and sign him out. He called his adult cousin, the same one that helped him obtain the firearm. Troy was expelled and ordered to family court to face the state solicitor, whom he describes as the one "trying to burn you" and get the "most time for the state" (Troy, 2014). He elaborates and reemphasizes that the solicitor is the one "Trying to get you messed up! One day the solicitor stopped by my home and talked to my mom and found out everything there is to know about me. Everything!" (Troy, 2014). Despite the solicitor sharing personal details about his life, the judge showed lenience and said that Troy seemed like an "intelligent and smart young man" and did not want to see him taken out of the care of his father. Troy maintains he could have received a *juvenile life sentence.*

Despite a promising verdict, he says he reached a point when he "just didn't care" (Troy, 2014). He left the state for three months and did not make contact with his parents. The day he finally decided to call his mother, she notified him that he was required in South Carolina for a court date. At that hearing, it was determined that Troy violated the terms of his probation (how he did this specifically is unknown), but it required eight months of "juvey" which he served right before his seventeenth birthday. He was unable to return to school because of the gun charge. He found himself in front of the same judge who had shown him leniency before. Troy paraphrases what the judge told him that day:

> So the judge looked at me again! Same woman, same lawyer. 'You will be 18 soon and all I am asking you to do is finish probation. Do what you're supposed to do and in three months you come back and see me and I'll take you off. The way you're going, if this don't wake you up, not putting you back into jail until you turn 18, I'll tell you the real prison system is going to get you. If you don't straighten up your act and do what you're supposed to do, they'll get you.' She was right (2014).

Troy heeded the advice and did not break his probation again for the duration of this period. He also says that he has been drug-free for well over a year, but did not focus on his sobriety until much later. I ask about the young man he believes set him up in high school. Troy tells me that he makes contact with his mother every now and then, but the young man is serving life in a federal prison. He adds that he does not associate with people that sell drugs and is grateful to be alive considering five separate occasions he had a gun pointed at his head by individuals looking to steal his drugs or money. His only regret is that he did not reach out to his father more, and says that their relationship has never been the same since the day he was caught selling drugs in school. When asked if there is anything he could have done differently to avoid the trouble that began in high school, he reflects and repeats the following three times: "I didn't say nothin. I didn't say nothin...I did not say nothin…I never sat down with my dad; I think that if I had said something a whole lot sooner and it would have also put some initiative behind some things I needed to do on my part, to meet him and my mom half way. That is what I regret. That's it" (2014).

Near the end of the interview, he adds that it took a few years to understand and 'learn' about his self, and learn to deal with problems in a sober way. Today, Troy says he faces his problems with a great deal of faith in God and that "I just don't see how to do it any other way" (2014).

Troy acknowledges that he willfully broke the law by selling drugs on school grounds. What is noteworthy about his violation is how he was caught and where he was caught, as well as who may have reported him. The terms of his arrest are somewhat suspicious, especially if what he states is true about the other young man facing minor consequences and never being mentioned in his court proceedings or being documented in court documents. He knew it was illegal to sell drugs, but did not realize the veracious implications of doing so in South Carolina. Finally, there is an economic and cultural difference in how he bought and sold marijuana before coming to South Carolina. Before moving to SC, he explained that he and friends bought and sold marijuana in a circle of private exchanges. This allowed he and his friends to rotate marijuana varieties, sometimes making a little profit if one variety was of better quality than another. This was a somewhat safe exchange that allowed everyone to "stay high" and keep some money in their pocket with minimal risk (Troy, 2014). Essentially,

Troy was accustomed to having a trusted circle of marijuana smokers to exchange with; this is also why he remained incident free before moving to SC. In many respects, he was unprepared for the disloyalty of the alleged informant and the consequences of getting caught by police.

Jamon

Jamon learned about Construct, SC from a friend that was removed from the program at some point. His decided to pursue the program without his friend. Jamon describes his experience at High School A and how his friends often encouraged him to consider attending college. He explains, "A friend asked me if I was going college. I told him 'no' and he told me I needed to go cause I am going need the degree" (Jamon, personal communication, May 2014). His friends were thinking long-term but he believed college would be a "waste" of time. Jamon fled positive peer-pressure and middle school classrooms due to his dislike of sitting or remaining still at a desk for a long period of time. More so, he connects the dislike of sitting to a critical incident involving a substitute teacher, about which he provides no details other than "I believe I left because of the substitute" (2014). When he left the class, he went to the gym to play basketball alone. Leaving class progressed to skipping and eventually chronic absenteeism, during which time he says he "really didn't care," (Jamon, 2014). He recalls that he made less effort to complete his schoolwork when attending High School A. In ninth grade, he explains: "What they were teaching, I hadn't been understanding. And they weren't helping, so I got frustrated and didn't do the work. So I stopped going to the class" (Jamon, 2014). He adds, "They're all the same, it's just that some teachers help more than others" (Jamon, 2014).

The first disciplinary action in response to his "skipping" was what is known as ISS, the abbreviated term for *In-School Suspension.* According to his recollection, ISS required no schoolwork and involved no activities. He describes simply sitting and doing no work. Based on his experiences, he offers this description of being suspended in school:

> When you're in class you're with other kids, and if your teacher didn't bring any work for you to do, you'd just sit in there all day. So you go to lunch and then you go back in there all day. Because it wasn't mandatory that we get our work. They didn't have to give it to us because we were supposed to be in class (2014).

Jamon describes attempts his father made to guide him to better decision-making, but that he did not listen because he received "referrals almost everyday" and was otherwise displaying *incorrigible*[23] behavior (2014). Jamon does not explain the reasons for getting so many referrals. It is possible he did not listen because he received so many, or alternatively, he did not listen thus causing him to be given referral(s). The support is from his father who he

---

[23] *Incorrigible* is an adjective describing a person or tendency not able to be corrected, improved, or reformed. In Sumter County, "Incorrigibility" ranked third on DJJ's top five referrals offenses in 2013.

describes as a man that had a good job and made a decent living. Jamon explains that his idea of a 'good job' is working in any sort of plant. As it turns out, his father worked at a large corporate plant before an injury placed him on disability.

Before CSC, Jamon describes three incidents involving the police. The first was in high school when he thought he could successfully steal money locked within a vehicle. A neighbor observed his attempt to break in and called the police. I ask him to tell me the story and he proceeds to describe how it all happened. *How did it feel being chased by police?* He describes it as "kind of fun" and an experience that gave him a "rush" but a thrill that dissolved when he realized he was about to be tased. Local officers gave him a break, he says; they decided not to charge the minor but to simply allow his father to pick him up. He describes his father being especially upset, but picking him up and taking him home nonetheless.

At seventeen, Jamon was selling candy with his brother when his sibling vocalized dissatisfaction directly with a woman who declined to purchase candy from them. Consequently, the woman called the police, which led to the young men being frisked for weapons. Jamon says, "They asked if I had any weapons on me or anything. They started patting me down and then found marijuana. Gave me a ticket and let me go, but in court they asked me what I was doing with the marijuana. I told her I smoked it. So she put me in a drug class and then I had to pay. I had to pay $600 and some change once I completed the class" (Jamon, 2014). The class, he said, was a "waste" of time.

The third incident is similar in that police had to frisk Jamon once again and found marijuana and crack cocaine. He admits that he'd been hanging out in a drug area when police rode by him a couple of times: "I been walking off and they stopped me and asked me what I was doing there and stuff. They asked me if I had my ID. I didn't think I had it, but when I looked in my pocket I did have it. Then he [police officer] says 'Oh, you're lying to me' and put me in handcuffs. Then they started searching me, found the drugs, and locked me up" (Jamon, 2014). He said he was "mad" (as he had stated earlier in our interview) and, again, his father was disappointed with his behavior. I ask him if he can confirm whether he was selling crack cocaine in addition to marijuana for income. He confirms by stating, "At that time I was not getting disability anymore," which I infer as his way of explaining a need for money at the time (2014). Additionally, he has experienced a mild neurological condition that "did not affect school" or learning, but was significant enough to provide supplemental income for a period of time.

Chris

Chris' earliest childhood memories are of moving. He has lived in and out of Sumter County for many years and attended many of its schools. He tells me his favorite school was a Christian school in another county in South Carolina. He smiles, saying "It was probably the best school I ever went to…. we ate on a table like on [the film] *Matilda*," he laughs and, continuing to smile, "I never knew the name of it" (Chris, personal communication, May 2014). He describes the pedagogical style of the schools and recalls the teachers were "way more" hands on, "like way hands on" and that each child was academically addressed and nurtured. It looked like a cathedral in the inside and children had their own workspace. This is where he began building and practicing his vocabulary:

> I started practicing vocabulary. 'Cause they made us [students] memorize the *Declaration of Independence* and I'd never memorized any literature that was that long. So after that, I felt, I realized I could learn words and just memorize them. After that, I just took that and started going with it. I pretty much picked that up and if pretty much, I picked that up from them, if they hadn't pushed me to do that, I would never really tried (Chris, 2014).

All of the children attending the school were dealing with hurt and pain, but were really happy at the same time, he remembers. Chris affirms that he never had any trouble in school with the exception of attendance; this caused him to be suspended and expelled more than once. Teachers were surprised he was advanced in mathematics, asking "'How do you know that? You ain't supposed to be on that yet!'" He goes on to say, "I had all A's for a long time, until attendance - I didn't know attendance affected your grade. So then my mom said, 'See you didn't go, you weren't there.' See, so then they expel and suspend. See I just didn't go" (2014).

Chris explains he often did not want to go to public school because he often stuck out and was criticized for how he speaks and that he was also the new kid, which often attracted unfavorable attention. When attending a school out-of-state, he describes being attacked while waiting for public transit on his first day home from school. After the incident, the police implicated him as a gang member, which he thought was preposterous. Chris describes seeing the "big" group walking toward him and realized he was in trouble:

> They walked up in a big group. How I knew they were coming to jump me because everyone had one [color][24] from head to toe. About twenty or thirty of them…they didn't really have [school] bus stops, so it was like city bus stops… I was on the curb. They thought I was selling drugs and were like, 'You're on our curb. And you ain't with us.' I am thinking *I am catching the bus. I didn't know this was anyone's curb. I don't even want to be catching this bus.* I am just standing, pacing back and forth trying to learn the bus schedule, trying to learn how I am even going to get home. I am glad they did that [jumped me] cause I got a ride home from the police. It was so far, I probably would have taken that bus and gotten lost. I mean that is just how it was 'cause every other curb is like a different gang; not like down here where they have this gang or that gang and that gang. It's just a lot of gangs, so you may be a part of this gang, but you're not from *that* street (2014).

---

[24] Omitted so not to implicate any persons or groups based on personal narrative.

When asked if he was ever hurt in an altercation, he exclaims, "I got cut! Yeah! They stabbed me a couple of times, it was like…" and he stops to show me the scars (2014). He tells me then how he came to understand gang culture and race relations in the north. When I ask the difference he offers that, "Down here [South Carolina] it is the government that is racist. It's the same everywhere, but down here you may be better off. 'Cause there is more black people down here and it is more common down here" (2014). The bias in the north, he says, is more individual, not only in a context of black and white.

Chris says his behavior almost got him *juvenile life*, which means being locked up in jail until at least twenty-one years of age. He was charged with *attempted murder* when, holding a knife, he threatened a young woman he believed to be an intruder. He says he reacted this way because his family moved to the community only weeks before. When Chris' mother saw him with the knife, she grabbed it and the young woman ran from the house. The incident was reported and by the time the police were called, he learned that the young woman was a friend of an older sibling. He recalls "I thought this person had broken into the house. They [she] didn't say anything and I was like, 'What are you doing in here?'"(2014). The two charges combined made him eligible for juvenile life, but when he was in front of the judge, she "somehow" understood the circumstance (Chris, 2014). At the time of this incident, Chris was ten years old, in fifth grade, and justifiably could have been sentenced to "eleven years or more" under juvenile law.

As our conversation comes to a close, Chris uses the term "systems" and "set-up" to describe repeated cycles of offending he has observed in others and himself (2014).

It didn't make me worser, because I realized that it can make you worse. If I were to go out again and mess up they have it set up to where, every time you get time, you get more time, I just thought about that… But other people don't think like that, they just be mad" (2014).

Chris says that he cannot get a summer job because of his record, which should already be expunged since he is at least eighteen years old now. I ask, then whether it has been expunged and he replies, "Nope, I was supposed to find out the other day but at the office [court], they said that I had to wait and come back" (2014).

Key Critical Statements & Insights

School Removal

Four out of the five interviewees describes excessive school suspensions or more than one expulsion. Each young man demonstrated changes in their vocal intonations, and body language when discussing their last memories of school. In two cases specifically, their statements were (I paraphrase): it was exhausting and I was really tired of trying to make it. One young man said he was tired of being kicked out. In these two cases, they were, in other words, fatigued.

The reasons for their removal may seem straightforward at times; however, there is room for interpretation. For instance, Mitchell was disheartened that having fun with a friend in the hall was seen as fighting or a serious disruption. Perhaps the teacher asked the young men repeatedly to stop and they did not. Maybe Mitchell's friend said or did something that the teacher found troubling enough to involve the principal and perhaps Mitchell did not know or the teacher did not say. The point here is there are a number of situational nuances to consider. Furthermore, the interviews are based on the men's past recollection and their perspective now - thus we cannot assume that each situation described accurately reflects the other party it involves (e.g., the teacher, Mitchell's friend, etc.).

Another example is Donald's frustration with not being able to take the GED test before he enrolled in the Construct, SC program. Donald recalled his commitment to getting his GED, but that he became frustrated at not being able to take the real test. There could have been a perfectly good reason, in addition to scoring low on the pre-test, why the adult education center did not allow him to take it. Donald may have been overly anxious or aggravated by having to walk to the adult education center everyday. If this was the case, which I cannot say for certain it was, then it is possible he did become frustrated either because he was not prepared or overtaxed by the regular attendance requirement.

Alternatively, it is just as plausible that he may have been discouraged from taking the test if he scored low on the pre-test. GED testing is an expense[25] to both the test-taker and the testing center. Although there are discounts available for those that qualify, or low cost risks, there could be testing implications for a testing center should unprepared applicants be permitted to take the test and fail.

Critical Statement: South Carolina's Prevailing 'White-Black' Binary[26]

A young man was led to discuss labeling and stereotypes in Sumter County during his interview. The discussion points further led him to share insights on racism, the local police and professional classes. Ultimately, the interview excerpt is about how he recognizes power as being retained and exercised by a small minority at the micro-level.

---

[25] http://www.gedtestingservice.com/testers/policy_sc#retesting
[26] Leonardo (2012).

Cause you've got crooked cops, knowing that they are harassing people and most of the cops are white. And that is where they [white people] get over at [over us]... a mayor or detective, they're all white. I ain't know. Like *everybody* over *anything*, like a councilor, is white. So basically, they just doing stuff to benefit themselves and their family and they're the rich type. I don't see them come around Sumter yet to fix up nothing yet for the blacks yet. Other than these roads, with potholes and stuff. They doing a little building, but it's not like they building homes for homeless people and stuff like that. They ain't thinking like that, they just taking lots of money and making new buses and roads and stuff and building stores and stuff."

The statement reveals the young man's view of power dynamics in Sumter County and how the dynamics affect his part of the city. He sees it widely separated by race and class, and that divisions in relation to both maintain a status quo of power. As he observes, police, politicians and educational professionals are mostly white and predominately in power. He sees a world dominated by a White professional class and that they have power to arrest, fix roads, and to help children in school, of course, if they *choose*. He is unconvinced the needs of people in less affluent communities like the one he comes from are a priority. As he states, the most basic upkeep, such as fixing a damaged road, is not done because it would mean sharing resources with low-income people.

The young man sees himself as a *rights-holder* and white educated professionals as *duty-bearers*[27]. However, beyond the White-Black binary in which he sees this, there is a general sense that those in command of resources are responsible to manage them impartially. Duncan Green (2012) articulates that, "These duty-bearers in turn have a responsibility to respect, protect, and fulfill the rights of 'rights-holders.' Rights, therefore, are naturally bound up with notions of citizenship, participation, and power." But we know that these relationships are broken in South Carolina racially, educationally, and politically. The fractures are historic, yet visible in the same institutions some believe were amended during the American Civil Rights Movement (e.g., public education [28]).

Critical Statement About Columbia Infamous Broad River Road Correctional Campus

"I was from the other side of the track, [they would have said] I want *him* to do 'JUVUY LIFE'… and when he gets out on his 18th birthday, go ahead and give *him five more years and send him to F1-Wing on SCDC.* That is where most of the juveniles that completed their 'juvenile time' go when they are eighteen years old. When they [juveniles] become an adult, at eighteen, they send them to some kind of prison or correctional facility for that age [group]. 'Cause once they are eighteen, they can't be in a juvenile facility. And they

---

[27] Rights-holder/Duty-Bearer concepts in Duncan Green's *Poverty to Power - How Active Citizens and Effective States Can Change the World (*2012).
[28] Example 1: Clarendon School District 1 in Clarendon County, SC, famous for Briggs vs. Elliot; example 2 is George Stinney murder trail.

continue the rest of their sentence through Adult Time" - CSC Interviewee (May, 2014).

This is how one interviewee described what could have happened to him when he went to court and stood in front of a judge. He describes how easy it is for a judge to sentence a young person, and first offender, to a juvenile life sentence, and more so, the incremental stages of confinement a young person can expect when and should this sentence is ruled. The young man understood that there was a perception of privilege and notes that this may have played a part of him not being ordered to serve a juvenile life sentence. It further suggests that a youth without advocates and resources is likely to face F1-Wing on SCDC (Broad River Road, Columbia, SC jail).

A judge or police officer gave me a 'break'

Chris and Troy note that a judge 'understood' their predicament, but before facing the judge believed they would face harsh consequences for their actions. Both remark that they *could have* been given juvenile life sentence, which would have assuredly kept them incarcerated until twenty-one years of age. One was for selling drugs on school property and the other for threatening bodily harm to another student. Also, in Jamon's interview he cites that the police opted to call his father rather than arrest him and send him to SCDJJ.

This past June, I was afforded to the opportunity to discuss juvenile delinquency in the state with a long-time SCDJJ employee.

Another Community Center employee and myself walked the SCDJJ employee to the door and engaged in small talk along the way. The SCDJJ employee discussed improvements in the agency's operations and how she and other department employees had worked diligently over the last ten years to increase preventative programs and advocated to judges to provide alternative programs before jail. Some of the SCDJJ programs include, "alternative marine, wilderness, and special treatment programs, which offer services in lieu of commitment or revocation for juveniles on probation or parole. Juveniles in these programs are on transfer, probation, or parole" (SCDJJ, 2014).

The SCDJJ employee also provided statistics that were indeed impressive, but could not be validated for this research paper. The employee noted that there have been substantial reductions in youth incarceration over the last five to seven years; this could be substantiated in a state agency press release nearly five years ago. A 2010 press release from the SCDJJ reported an "all-time low of its incarcerated population going from 431 youth in 2003 to 195 in August 2010… indicators that effective new DJJ reforms are having a positive impact on the juvenile justice system in South Carolina" (SCDJJ, 2010).

Sumter County Livelihood[29]

Young adults enrolled in Construct, US (CUSA) have limited resources including income, transportation, technology and, in some cases, reliable shelter. In addition, many enrollees face legal trouble that may sometimes continue long after an incident has occurred. These typically require resources that they either do not have or have very little of (time, money, legal representation, or mobility). In the occurrence of other 'shocks' and given limited resources, they can sometimes depart from the program for weeks at a time (Green, 2012). Basic resources that are unavailable or seem *unattainable* can stir frustrations, thus affecting outlook and motivation. This was captured in two interviews where the young men described having to walk in the South Carolina heat, one saying he would appreciate a vehicle because it is *too hot to be out in the sun*[30]. There is no reliable transportation besides taxis and although a transportation center exists, it is underutilized and regarded as unreliable.

Trusted Authority Figures

The attitudes I observed of the staff toward CSC young people might represent the attitudes they face outside the Community Center. Their scrutiny likely comes from a place of caring, but they seem unable or untrained to take that and transform

---

29 Vulnerability to sudden 'shocks', the result both of individual or social factors (gender, age, disability, health, class, or caste) and of the relative power of an individual or community to defend their interests, is one of the defining characteristics of poverty.

[30] Heat is cited as one of the leading weather-related killer in the United States, resulting in hundreds of fatalities each year (National Weather Service [NWS], June 20, 2014).

in it a way that uplifts the young person. As at least five different enrollees mentioned in some way, *he doesn't think I'm ready [to work]* or *he wants me to cut my hair [to get a job]* and *she told me I wasn't serious [because I missed classes].* The CSC staff quickly earns the trust of new program participants, but can quickly squander it because of frustrations they perceive about the young people. This is also a figurative fault line that can offset young people, and also their effort to get back on a steady educational course.

Culpability

Each young man interviewed for this study took personal responsibility for actions that led to or contributed to being removed from school, arrested, or incarcerated. Not one young man participated in a tirade that blamed other people for their mistakes: White people, rich people or even "picky" teachers, many of whom are referenced as Black. I asked each participant, at least once, to reconsider one situation that derailed him some how and what he could have done differently (e.g., *What other options did you have? How would you describe that specific response?*). This question often led to straight admissions and alternative decision-making he could have made, had he known then what he knows now. Mind you, their admissions do not exempt the experience they had, as in what he saw, how he felt, and the recollections. In other words, if Mitchell found his teacher picking on him "all the time" then this should not be viewed as Mitchell victimizing himself. Simply, that was his experience, at that time and with that specific teacher

(Mitchell, personal communication, May 2014). As a reminder, during the interview Mitchell assumed responsibility for not going back to school because he wanted to avoid altercations like the one he had with his girlfriend. He also felt that going back to school made him more likely to get in trouble or more specifically, led to his incarceration.

Lest we forget, school removal and correctional tradition is rampant in South Carolina and often irrationally enforced. In 2013, The New York Daily News reported a story from South Carolina that headlined "Overreaction? 6-year-old South Carolina girl is expelled from school after bringing plastic toy gun to class," (Ortiz, 2013). A kindergartner named Naomi McKinney brought her brother's clear, plastic toy gun to class and was kicked out of school. Her parents were notified in a letter if she were "caught on school grounds she'll be 'subject to the criminal charge of trespassing,'" (Ortiz, 2013). These circumstances are uncommon, but show to what length a South Carolina public schools exercise authority in the most innocent of circumstances.

'Quiet' Dysfunction

There is another culture in Sumter County that was found to be as common as correctional reform, and that is the culture of being *quiet* or simply not speaking up. For instance, one grievance of the Director was that no one was communicating with her and that it was frustrating when she observed situations that, in order to be resolved, required the discussion and feedback of her staff.

In my conversations with staff, *each one* began in neutral terms about their work and morale, including their relationship with the Director. There was a lot of *it's good,* or *we all work together...* but when asked specific questions about *their* experience, *their* problem-solving in certain situations and their leadership style, specific details surfaced. Overall, I saw that all intended to keep the working environment peaceful, but in trying to do so it backfired. There were resentments; anxieties, anger, and frustrations were discussed at a meeting that I facilitated after the interviews were over. There were teachers that felt overworked or felt that they carried more of the program's burden than others. The program has clearly defined job roles for each staff member, but these were observed as being poorly followed. My suggestion during this time was to consider revisiting job descriptions and responsibilities, adjusting tasks if necessary and then setting clear expectations to move the group forward. I also suggested regularly scheduled meetings, opportunities for feedback and more written accounts of daily operations especially those in relation to Construct, SC enrollees (e.g., incident reports, progress reports, etc.).

Methodology

Participants

The sample groups were all over eighteen years of age and identify as male, African American and Sumter County residents. All have lived in the county for at least 10 years. The interview sample consisted of five enrollees, which meant that all were pursuing an educational degree or a trade certification due to some circumstance that left the young person unable or unwilling to return to public school. There was a selection effort in the beginning to obtain interviews from young men that have experienced all three institutional bodies, namely, public school, juvenile justice or state corrections and a non-profit entity, which in this case was the affiliate Construct, SC program. Selecting candidates that met this criterion did seem important at one time to understand whether they were as dominant in their lives as each first seemed. However, time constraints and sample availability became concerns that required an adjustment of my candidate criteria. The interviews were arranged without knowing if each candidate met the (original) criteria, of course with the exception of being CSC active participants. The candidates were approached with a letter of consent after the CSC staff and Director approved the researcher activities.

One candidate declined, but not directly to me or anyone else as far as I know. He said that he would consider it and was provided a letter of consent; a signed copy was never returned, however. In early readings, the study was confronted as being one-dimensional ina sense, because there was a lack of repeated reflection on my behalf restating each man's culpability in particular certain scenarios shared during the interview. However, each young man took responsibility for most all of his mistakes, even if he perceived bias from an authority or individual. In some descriptions in which the men reported trouble, details were withheld that offered a clearer view of the overall circumstance. For instance, one interviewee stated he was kicked out of gym class for drawing on his clothes; however, he was drawing symbols that associated him with a gang. The interviewee did not volunteer that he was drawing gang symbols, but did not hesitate to tell me what exactly he drew. We might also assume the principal was made aware that the symbols were gang-affiliated, but felt comfortable allowing the young man to leave his office without further consequence. Again, it is educated guesswork, but doing so may be more important to some readers of this study than others.

Procedures

I was the sole researcher and conducted five low-structured interviews. There was one interview that required more structured questioning to obtain a clearer understanding of the young man's experience. One interview objective was to understand the circumstances that led each young man to the Construct, SC program. The interviews ranged from low-to-semi-structured, depending on the interviewee. This permitted greater latitude in the kinds of answers the young men could provide because the overall goal was to find out what was relevant or most significant about their journey to CSC. It also allowed me to listen closely for markers because I found I was less concerned about getting through a list of questions. The interviews were recorded and jottings were taken to document physical responses, interruptions or verbal markers that seemed important to return to. This allowed me to adjust my line of questioning based on details that seemed most important to their narratives.

At the beginning of each interview, I revisited points that were contained in the letter and thanked the individual for their time. Each interview was conducted in a confidential area of the Community Center, after hours and with at least one staff member present in another area of the building.

In two cases I knew more about the interviewee than they may have realized. For instance, one young man witnessed the murder of his mother when he was a small child. The Director, who I found to show him a great deal of compassion, treated him thoughtfully and found resources (e.g., counseling) to cope and begin healing from the trauma. Another young man experienced frequent periods of homelessness, but never indicated this in his interview.

Analysis

The interviews were all transcribed and coded to identify themes and patterns in a sequential mixed method design (Hesse-Biber and Leavy, 2010). Critical ethnography was employed to understand the social life of the CSC constituency, who initially seemed *bullied out or in* to state institutions that govern education or reform bodies (juvenile justice, corrections, or non-profit organizations). Thus, I sought to research the men's narratives and reasoning behind certain behaviors and decision-making. The inquiry recognized the young men's culpability in many circumstances of their life, but sought explanation of the "partial truth" or "dominant ideology" that remains in the state reflecting hundreds of years of enslavement, as well as to other forms of structural violence on behalf of White southerners like peonage and vagrancy laws which all had a hand in crafting the dominant ideology (Hesse-Biber and Leavy, 2010). Based on the historical reports, events and statistical data today there is a dominant ideology that has developed about Black males in the state: Black males are in need of reform or "more discipline," as each staff member stated at least once in each interview at the beginning of my practicum (CSC staff, January 2014).

Interview Assessment Tables

Table 1: Elementary School-Age Experiences		
I had a positive elementary school experience		**Responses**
"Grammar. Being able to talk properly and read properly [as good things]." -P3	Agree	2
"There wasn't much I didn't like about elementary school." -P1	Neutral	3
"I'd move to a different school every month or two." -P2	Disagree	-
"Before the age of 10. My dad stayed talking a lot whenever he was around." -P5 "It was alright" -P4	No Response/Opinion	-
When I was a small child, I experienced situations that changed my outlook on education		**Responses**
"[Knew] That any kind of horseplay would not be accepted at all... It got bad at the end of elementary school... I'd miss months out of school." -P1	Agree	4
"I never said anything. It was some white dude in his daycare he was racist. I never knew he was racist, but I knew he never treated me the same as the white kids. And then one day he hit me. I was real, I was 4 years old and my mom was like 'Yo, your face looks swollen' and I was lying for him." -P2	Neutral	1
	Disagree	-
"He'd try and teach me about life, and you don't understand it then, cause you're young, but you're listening though. My dad wanted me to understand that there are people out here in this world that come into your life as friends, but they are not your friends." -P5	No Response/Opinion	-
"I was quieting sometimes, sad. Friendly." -P3		
"No [no none in elementary]." -P4		

Table 2: Middle School-Age Experiences		
In middle school my outlook and behavior declined due to new frustrations		**Responses**
"Good and bad. I started getting kicked out, like every year around the same time…I still been quiet every now and then. Noticeable. Bad. Suspensions, expulsions." -P3	Agree	4
"Bad, vicious want to hit people for no reason. A little bit of a bully. I got to bully the bullies. That is what I loved about school. I'd used to bully the bullies. They used to think they was bad, but I was bad."	Neutral	1
	Disagree	-
"It got bad in middle school and it got ad at the end of elementary school. In middle school I started skipping" -P1	No Response/Opinion	-
"I was living life the correct way. Like nothing, no type of habits, or distractions came into my life yet." -P5		
"Just go [somewhere else] sit down and probably play basketball" - P4		
"Especially at 13 and 14 that is when everything got crazy."		
"Down here it was like 'You talk like a white person' I'd hear that so much to the point I picked up slang." -P2		
When I started skipping Middle School classes…		**Responses**
"I started cutting the same class. Probably about three or four times…I think 13. " - P4	Agree	3
"I started skipping school in fifth grade." -P3		
"I never had any problems with any people, look at my school record. I never had no problems, *but* truancy. I just never wanted to be around the other students." -2	Neutral	-
	Disagree	2
"School wasn't going to put any money in my pocket, with the exception of allowances for getting a good report card." P1	No Response/Opinion	-
"I never stopped going" -P5		

Table 3: High School-Age Experiences		
I feel responsible for not graduating from a public school in The County or surrounding Counties		**Responses**
"I was in a rebellious stage... School more of a place that I wanted to go to get away from home." -P5 "I felt different."-P2 "He [father] told me to stop cutting class and to do what I need to do before I get kicked out. Didn't listen, kept on doing it. I got kicked out." -P4 "I was afraid of going back to jail because of going back to Sumter High." -P1 "You could never get me in trouble cause I never talked... I am the kind of person to do my work and put my head down." -P3	Agree	3
	Neutral	2
	Disagree	-
	No Response/Opinion	-
I experienced disciplinary action in high school which was appropriate or justifiable in most cases.		**Responses**
"[I can't remember, I know it's too many."P3 "First time in adult jail." -P3 "Something happened. I wasn't going to school; I went back to the alternative school... It just felt different, so everything stopped. Stopped going to school." - P3 "ISS, In-School Suspension." P4 "Referred me to alternative school" "Then I'd get write up, suspended, come back and still do the same thing." -P4 "Tired of being written up" -P1 "They took me to jail" -P1 "I notice a kid that might be bad or may get expelled a lot. - P4 "Wrote me ticket." P1 "Supposed to do home schooling cause I couldn't go back because of the [omitted] charge and all that" -P5 "That is why I am going through this little thing now, still in school messing up. That's why I am running from them." - P1	Agree	-
	Neutral	5
	Disagree	-
	No Response/Opinion	-
There was one or more parental figures that always tried to steer me in the right direction		**Responses**
"She cared about the education. I actually did home schooling. She had a lot of books too, so I kind of did it [learn] myself. Cause I didn't want to go to school." -P2 "My dad is still holding an old grudge, my dad loves me to death, and my dad still helped me... he helped me." -P5 "She helped me get out of jail. She showed me that she cared, cause my grandmother wasn't going to get me out. I got locked before my test and if I was still locked up and wouldn't have been able to take the test and probably wouldn't have my GED right now." -P3 "We ever followed up on it... We still close. But we don't have that bond." -P4	Agree	5
	Neutral	-
	Disagree	-
	No Response/Opinion	-

88

"She already knew... 'Yes, ma'am.' She said, 'Don't bring all them hoodlums back to my house neither.'" -P1		

Table 4: All the Experiences In-Between Elementary Through High School		
I recall moments when I felt wronged/insulted/overlooked by authority a child should trust		**Responses**
"They're all the same, it's just that some teachers help more than others." -P4 "Cause she was a picky teacher, just *picking* for no reason. "If I was wearing a certain style, she'd say 'What do you have your shirt like that, take it down.' Like you can't tell me how to wear my clothes.'" -P1 "I cannot *beeelieve* what I heard her say, I won't even tell you." - P3 "Before even court started, they are sitting there joking...I am like 'Hello! You laughing with her and stuff? This is serious!" -P5	Agree Neutral Disagree No Response/Opinion	4 1 - -
I was fatigued by my public school and correctional experiences in South Carolina		**Responses**

"Something happened. I wasn't going to school; I went back to the alternative school…It just felt different, so everything stopped. Stopped going to school." -P3	Agree Neutral	5 -
"A couple of weeks later I called up there and he said I couldn't come back. I just thought if they ain't gonna schedule a meeting than forget it. Then I ain't going back no more. I stopped caring less. I started talking back, cussing and stuff. -P4	Disagree No Response/Opinion	- -
"That's how I was like 'Awe, man. Life going to be life'…but every job now wants a GED or diploma." -P1		
"I didn't have any drugs on me, and didn't do nothing, I didn't have any drugs on me. I just was at some family member's house and they do that, but I just got caught in a drug bust...they slammed me. That is how they handle you, they like pick up, slam you on the ground, put cuffs on you and put their knees in your back and type thing." -P2		

Table 5: My current track		
I aspire to…	**In order to…**	**So that I may one day…**
To remain clear and focused on my making the most of my gifts	I can use my personal writing to develop scripts for film	So I can one day retire on food by owning a restaurant.
Complete a college degree become a lucrative business man	Be a pillar in my community and honor my mother	Enjoy the fruits of my labor and help anyone that needs it any time.
Earn a ton of trade certifications, earn legal money in the future, and go to college	To start a small business in construction or landscaping, possibly a car wash	Purchase land and collect other people's rent checks, while on an island he bought along with his own mansion.
To work and complete a college degree	Start my own recycling business	To be successful in my work
Remain at peace and happy	Listen more often than I talk	Be a college graduate

Table 6: Summary of Experiences	Definitive Yes Responses
Alternative Schools	5
Serious Charges	4
Obtained GED	3
College bound	3
Aspires to own a business	3
Reports at least being given a "major break" by a authority figure of correctional body	2
Reports at least one *illegal* activity to earn income	4
Reports at least one *informal legal* economic activity for income	5
Reports at least one *formal legal* economic activity for income	3
Reports positive outlook moving forward	5

91

Limitations of this Study

Early Beginnings

The fortuitous nature of my inquiry that began with early assignments to improve communication, prepare the staff for a transition in leadership and other concerns decreased opportunities that may have given me more time with program constituents. More time would have also provided me opportunities to build trust and increased the size of my sample, which I hoped would include six to eight young men as opposed to five.

Construct Staff

In hindsight, the study would have benefited from another set of interviews that would have allowed the staff that were born and raised in Sumter County to share their experiences as professionals outside of the Construct program. This would have been more inclusionary and valuable in understanding CSC as a non-profit authority and the staff as potential advocates for enrollees within the CSC program.

Conclusion

The institutional reform in South Carolina has and continues to impact the narratives of African American boys and men today. In public schools, reform culture is reflected in the high rates of disciplinary action taken against Black adolescents. In the juvenile and adult corrections systems, it is reflected in similar disproportionate referrals and incarceration rates, thus making correctional culture more prevalent in the lives of Black South Carolinians.

This research seeks to confirm that correctional culture is a part of South Carolina's state history and dates back as far as the mid-1870s during a time known as a radical Reconstruction of the South. From around the 1880s until the American Civil Rights Movement, research indicates that Black men and boys were not only undervalued by the state, but also exploited to little avail of their human value or personhood. Black men and children were placed on chain gangs and forced into farm labor, often whipped, chained and overworked into exhaustion or death, all for state profit.

Juvenile boys were excluded from receiving formal education, learning trades and also exploited for their labor. More importantly, they were neglected. We know they were forced to live in filth and that zero dollars were invested in them, not even for the most basic decencies (e.g., toothbrush, heating, clean bedding, etc.). Subsequently, generations of Black male children endured abuses that were not only physical, but assuredly had psychological effects for those in the Reformatory for Negro Boys. The critical perspective allows for understanding the historical subjugation in South Carolina and as outlined in this paper.

African American males are not oppressed or victims in recent history since the closing of the reformatory, but they are left with residual damages of racism upheld scant generations ago. The narrative accounts of the young men in CSC show the socioeconomic vulnerabilities that challenge them in their effort to uplift themselves educationally and vocationally. CSC constituents that are most determined find their way to either a two- or four-year college. The dominant ideology currently in South Carolina is young Black males are challenged solely by individual character flaws (e.g., lack of seriousness or lazy habits of dress, etc.). The wide acceptance of this ideology undermines meaningful efforts to understand achievement gaps as well as disproportionate school delinquency and correctional actions in the lives of South Carolina's African-American populace.

Looking ahead, there is an author named E. Hammond Oglesby that writes primarily in the Christian tradition, yet often remarks on the political fight for 'freedom' and 'humanity' given African-American history of 'black exclusion' (1999, 122). I agree with the author's point that separation and marginalization is this country's most profound ethical dilemma (Oglesby, 1999, p. 123).

I propose that schools in South Carolina consider an engagement model and forgo the correctional language and procedures that are so prevalent in their procedures. According to the

Medical University of South Carolina, the engagement model is an 'evidence-based' approach to treating patients and consists of 'healing' or 'engaging' languages in the delivery of "trauma-informed care" (Medical University of South Carolina [MUSC], 2014). In many respects, such an approach or even a revised version could benefit middle school age children because statistics and interview data show Black boys 13-15 as most vulnerable to being removed. One of these alternative programs which implements a type of engagement model approach is a non-profit named AMIkids Piedmont.[31] The organization uses youth development approaches, such as bonding, gender responsiveness, high expectations for success, and cultural exploration (AMIkids, Inc., 2012).

However, school districts seem most capable of effectively reframing disciplinary procedures so that it is not as corrections-intensive as it is now. Districts might also consider the 'Counterspace' framework that seeks to improve psychological well-being in groups that are marginalized by race, gender or class, as it is through this framework that groups can unite in a "community of others" (Hunter & Case, 2012, p. 261). Instead of in-school suspensions or chronic removal, narrative work could very well be a process that "brings about healing and restoration to marginalized individuals through contesting pejorative societal representations relative to these individuals and their reference groups" (Case & Hunter, 2012, p. 262). I believe my research shows that each

---

[31] AMIkids Piedmont operates by the values and standards of AMIkids, Inc. and creates an environment in which students of all types can learn and thrive. A referral center of SCDJJ (amikidspiedmont.org/our-services/what-we-do/).

interviewee found his own way of contesting the pejorative representations in society.

Bibliography

Alexander, Michelle (2012). The New Jim Crow (p. 199). New Press, The Kindle Edition.

Anderson, Thom, (2012). *COLUMN: Industrial School for Boys: Pee Dee's first state institution,* Retrieved June 12, 2014, from http://www.scnow.com/opinion/article_8f34de18-0d63-52a5-ac50-fad433d6b0e9.html#.U7rlydIyIXI.gmail

Baker, R. (2011, February 23). Briggs v. Elliott: Summerton schools still mostly segregated. *The Sumter Item.*

Bolton, W. (2013, July 23). Bolton: Black men endure a lifetime of suspicion. Message posted to read more here: http://www.thestate.com/2013/07/23/2874995/bolton-black-men-endure-a-lifetime.html#storylink=cpy

Case, A., & Hunter, C. (2012). Counterspaces: A unit of analysis for understanding the role of settings in marginalized individuals' adaptive responses to oppression. *American Journal of Community Psychology, 50*(1), 257-270.

Green, D. (2012). *From power to poverty: How active citizens and effective states can change the world* (Second ed.). Warwickshire CV23 9QZ, UK: Practical Action Publishing.

Hart, H. H. (1918). *The war program of the state of South Carolina, A report prepared at the request of governor Richard I. Manning, the state council of defense and the state board of charities and corrections.* Quarterly Bulletin. New York City: Russell Sage Foundation. (War Program of the State of South Carolina).

Hathitrust Digital Library. (2014). *Http://catalog.hathitrust.org/Record/002131512.* Retrieved June 30, 2014 from http://catalog.hathitrust.org/Record/002131512

Jamon. (2014). In Krejčí-Shaw A. (Ed.), *Personal communication.*

Kinnard, M. (2007, January 29). Iraqis get ideas from S.C. prisons. *The Washington Post.*

Kulmala, T. (2013). *Report: S.C. first in rate of women murdered by men.* Newspaper Article Aiken Standard.

Leonardo, Z. (2012). The race for class: Reflections on a critical raceclass theory of education. *Educational Studies: Journal of the American Educational Studies Association, 48*(5), 427-449.

McCord, C. H. (January 1, 1914). *The American negro as a dependent, defective and delinquent* (1st ed.). Nashville, Tennessee: Press of Benson Printing Company.

McWhorter, J. (2014). *'Microaggression' is the new racism on campus.* Retrieved March 21, 2014 from http://time.com/32618/microaggression-is-the-new-racism-on-campus/

National Geographic Society. (October 28, 2010). *In U.S. South, Textile Mills Gone but Not Forgotten.* Retrieved June 20, 2014 from http://news.nationalgeographic.com/news/2004/10/1019_04101 9_textile_mills_2.html

Ortiz, Erik. (January 31, 2013) *Overreaction? 6-year-old South Carolina girl is expelled from school after bringing plastic toy gun to class.* Retrieved June 6, 2014 from http://www.nydailynews.com/news/national/s-student-6-expelled-plastic-toy-gun-article-1.1252179

Phillips, N. (September 25, 2013). *Men killing women: SC ranks 1st, again.* Retrieved June 7, 2014 from http://www.thestate.com/2013/09/25/3001145/south-carolina-worst-in-country.html

Right On Crime. (2010). *State initiatives: South Carolina.* Retrieved May 31, 2014 from http://www.rightoncrime.com/reform-in-action/state-initiatives/south-carolina/

South Carolina Department of Corrections. *A chronology of major Events/Developments.* Retrieved April 13, 2014 from http://www.doc.sc.gov/pubweb/about_scdc/AgencyHistory1.jsp

South Carolina Department of Corrections. (2014). *Profile of inmates in institutional count (including inmates on authorized absence) as of June 2013* SCDOC.

South Carolina Board of Charities and Corrections. (1915). *First annual report.* Columbia, South Carolina: Gonzalas and Brian State Printers. Retrieved from HathiTrust Digital Library.

The PEW Charitable Trusts. (2013). *Public safety performance project.* Retrieved May 14, 2014 from

http://www.pewtrusts.org/en/research-and-analysis/fact-

sheets/2013/01/14/public-safety-in-south-carolina

The Sentencing Project. (2014). *U.S. trends in corrections, 1925-*

2012. Issue Brief. Washington DC: The Sentencing Project.

Trotti, J. L. *Brief history of juvenile justice in South Carolina.*

Retrieved March 30, 2014 from

http://www.state.sc.us/djj/history.php

Appendices

Images are captured from online sources cited in Bibliography unless otherwise noted

Appendix 1: Sumter County Population by Employment/Unemployment

	Sumter County			South Carolina			United States		
Year	Employment	Unemp.	Rate	Employment	Unemp.	Rate	Employment	Unemp.	Rate
2010	40,146	5,416	11.9	1,922,815	241,797	11.2	139,064,000	14,825,000	9.6
2009	39,668	5,617	12.4	1,928,110	246,794	11.3	139,877,000	14,265,000	9.3
2008	40,172	3,612	8.2	1,998,171	145,617	6.8	145,352,000	8,924,000	5.8
2007	41,352	3,108	7.0	2,000,185	119,245	5.6	146,047,000	7,078,000	4.6
2006	42,199	3,520	7.7	1,970,912	134,123	6.4	144,427,000	7,001,000	4.6
2005	42,353	3,959	8.5	1,922,367	139,983	6.8	141,730,000	7,591,000	5.1
2004	41,987	3,556	7.8	1,888,050	138,430	6.8	139,252,000	8,149,000	5.5
2003	41,287	3,338	7.5	1,854,419	133,257	6.7	137,736,000	8,774,000	6.0
2002	39,572	3,098	7.3	1,826,240	115,907	6.0	136,485,000	8,378,000	5.8
2001	40,330	2,824	6.5	1,834,871	100,743	5.2	136,933,000	6,801,000	4.7
2000	43,263	1,876	4.2	1,917,365	70,794	3.6	136,891,000	5,692,000	4.0

Source: S.C. Department of Employment & Workforce

Appendix 2: Sumter County Population by Age

Age Range	Sumter County	South Carolina	United States
0-4	8,018	297,806	20,860,364
5-9	7,276	283,181	19,863,359
10-14	7,531	293,587	20,590,895
15-19	7,634	321,107	21,542,504
20-24	8,933	305,221	21,163,659
25-29	7,055	300,373	20,863,904
30-34	5,882	279,567	19,579,299
35-39	6,368	295,814	20,785,318
40-44	7,185	314,800	21,963,256
45-49	7,258	321,140	22,728,145
50-54	6,917	306,165	20,918,627
55-59	5,960	278,181	18,098,647
60-64	4,915	240,424	14,502,706
65-69	3,934	180,709	10,892,799
70-74	3,268	135,910	8,703,233
75-79	2,849	112,685	7,472,931
80-84	1,858	83,448	5,778,062
85 and older	1,600	66,749	5,153,845
Total	**104,441**	**4,416,867**	**301,461,533**

Source: U.S. Census Bureau, American Community Survey   2009 5-Year Estimate

Appendix 3: Sumter County Population by Race

Race	Sumter County	%	South Carolina	%	United States	%
White	51,944	49.74	2,977,453	67.41	224,469,780	74.46
Black	49,180	47.09	1,245,855	28.21	37,264,679	12.36
American Indian/Alaskan Native	335	0.32	13,825	0.31	2,423,294	0.80
Asian	1,317	1.26	53,258	1.21	13,201,056	4.38
Native Hawaiian/ Other Pacific Islander	11	0.01	2,130	0.05	447,591	0.15
2 or more races	1,085	1.04	58,451	1.32	6,668,680	2.21
Other	569	0.54	65,895	1.49	16,986,453	5.63
Total	**104,441**		**4,416,867**		**301,461,533**	

Source: U.S. Census Bureau, American Community Survey   2009 5-Year Estimate

Appendix 4: Sumter County School District School Suspension

Report 2011-2012

Sumter School District
Suspension Report
Aug. 16, 2011 - May 31, 2012

SCHOOL	BLACK		WHITE		HISPANIC		ASIAN-AMERICAN		WHITE/BLACK		OTHER		TOTAL	Enrollment
	Male	Female	Male	Female	Male	Female	Male	Female	Male	Female	Male	Female		
Alice Dr Elem	25	3	5						1				34	683
Alice Dr Middle	108	52	16	2		1			1				180	760
Bates Middle	156	69	54	14	3				4		1		301	752
Cherryvale	26	7	6	1									40	459
Chestnut Oaks	159	72	10	2	2				1				246	517
Crestwood	293	175	29	17	6	3			7	5	5	5	545	1,164
Croswell	67	15	6	1		1							90	602
Ebenezer	58	40	13	2	4		1				2		120	362
FJ Delaine	2	1	1										4	133
Furman	77	30	55	20	1	1			1	4			189	941
High Hills	9	7	7			1			4				28	453
Hillcrest	52	14	23	9	3	1							102	463
Kingsbury	36	5	10	3	1								55	691
Lakewood	126	77	66	36					4				309	1,116
Lemira	56	15	1	1									73	557
Manchester	5	3	2	1									11	479
Mayewood	36	17	5										58	166
Millwood	13	2	10										25	670
Oakland	3	2	5	1	1				2				14	673
Pocalla	46	14	39	5									104	919
Rafting Creek	12		1										13	206
RE Davis	19	5	3										27	317
Shaw Heights	43	7	12	2	4				1		2		71	524
Sumter High	336	212	69	39	5		3		2		1		667	1,299
Wilder	17	3	3	2									25	450
Willow Dr	69	14			2	1							86	601
TOTALS	1,849	861	451	158	32	9	4	0	28	9	11	5	3,417	16,957
% of Totals	54.11%	25.20%	13.20%	4.62%	0.94%	0.26%	0.12%	0%	0.82%	0.26%	0.32%	0.15%		100.00%

Appendix 5: RFN and SCISB

CHAPTER X.

SOUTH CAROLINA INDUSTRIAL SCHOOL FOR BOYS.

This school was visited by the State Board of Charities and Corrections on November 11, 1919. At the time of our visit we found Mr. J. B. Johns, Superintendent, in charge. Since that date Mr. Johns has resigned and Dr. Charles H. Prince, who is in charge of the print shop, has been appointed Superintendent *pro tem*.

The Plant.—We found the buildings in fairly good condition, with the exception of the cottage that contains the dining room and kitchen. This is an old building and needs extensive repairs. We noted especially the decayed condition of the upstairs porch in the rear. The plumbing in all of the buildings appeared to us to be in working condition, and we like especially the toilet arrangements in the McCown Cottage. The beds in the McCown Cottage were clean and attractive looking; but those in the old building, in which there is the dining room, are of the antiquated double-decked type. The Superintendent assured us that he would replace them as soon as possible. We found the cow barn in a clean and sanitary condition.

Medical Facilities.—The arrangements for taking care of sick boys are meager and inadequate. There is no trained nurse employed, so when boys fall sick they have to rely upon what attention their school-fellows can give them. The new infirmary that is now building will be a great step forward, and we trust that it will have modern furnishings and be directed by a physician whose sole function at the school will be the care of the boys' bodies, and that it will be served by a trained nurse. On our visit to the school we found only two sick boys, and these did not seem to have serious ailments.

New Dining Hall and Kitchen.—This is nearing completion and makes a fine appearance. It is a brick structure with kitchen and playroom in the basement and dining hall on the first floor. The kitchen has already installed a modern bakery of the best type and

CHAPTER IX.

STATE REFORMATORY FOR NEGRO BOYS.

We visited this institution on December 24, and found 196 boys there. Since our last inspection the reformatory has established a school with two negro teachers of good character and of good ability. This school is making excellent progress in giving the boys the rudiments of an education and in influencing them through contact with good men of their own race. The schoolhouse was clean and very well arranged and equipped for a beginning.

The sleeping quarters, dining room and kitchen were all cleaner than we had ever seen them and they were decorated with holly for the Christmas season. We found the boys in good physical condition, not one being sick at the time of our visitation. The premises about the building were well kept.

We noted with pleasure a number of improvements: The guards' quarters had been rebuilt and painted, the old wooden building to the rear of the present dormitory was repaired and repainted on the inside for a school, the brick oven in the kitchen—so unsightly and so unclean—had been removed and a new range installed in its place, screens were in the windows and doors. Altogether there has been commendable improvement in the physical appearance of the place.

There is great need of a new building. So long as one building has to house all of the boys, there can be no proper classification of the inmates. All ages and all kinds of characters are herded in the same dormitory. So long as this state of affairs exists little real reformation may be expected among the boys. Indeed, such conditions as there obtain can only go towards making the ordinary boy vicious, and the vicious boy intolerably evil. We urge that this serious factor be given careful attention. Another detracting feature of the reformatory is that there are only 125 single beds for 190 boys, with the result that two boys often have to sleep together in a single bed. The sleeping quarters are over-crowded and because of this over-crowding, are unsanitary. This, too, urges us to recommend the erection of another building.

104

Appendix 6: First Annual Report

CHAPTER XIII.
STATE REFORMATORY FOR NEGRO BOYS

Located in Richland County, about five miles from Columbia on the Broad River Road; Mr. S. A. Lindsay, superintendent.

Administration.—The State Reformatory for Negro Boys was established in 1900, when it was put under the control of the Board of Directors of the State Penitentiary. By an Act of the General Assembly of 1918 this institution was placed under the direction of the Board of Correctional Administration and this Board took control on April 11, 1918. In 1920 the General Assembly abolished the Board of Correctional Administration and placed the Reformatory under the control of the State Board of Public Welfare. Dr. R. T. Jennings is physician for the Reformatory. Religious services are held every Sunday by Mr. A. T. Stratton, for many years secretary of the Y. M. C. A. at Columbia. An industrial instructor is employed, who teaches the boys shoemaking and carpentry. There are two negro teachers who instruct the boys in the rudiments of academic education and in morals. There are seven foremen that direct the boys in their work of the farm. The total number of officers and employees is thirteen, of whom nine are residents.

Admission.—The Reformatory receives by commitment all "male criminals, other than white boys, under 16 years of age, who shall be legally sentenced to said Reformatory on conviction of any criminal offense in any Court having jurisdiction thereof and punishable by imprisonment in the State Penitentiary." By Act No. 429, Acts 1912, Section 5, the Probate Court is given authority to commit to this Reformatory juvenile delinquents under 18 years of age. By this latter provision a great number of small boys have been committed to the institution.

Appendix 7: Sumter County - Types of Juvenile Case 2012-2013

Number and Types of Juvenile Cases

	County	State
Total Number of Juvenile Cases	289	16,754
Percent Increase/Decrease from Previous Year	-17%	-2%
Number of Juvenile Cases Classified as Violent or Serious	44	1,394
Percent Increase/Decrease from Previous Year	-8%	1%
Number of Status Offense Cases	26	1,409
Percent Increase/Decrease from Previous Year	136%	7%

Top Five Referral Offenses in Juvenile Cases

County		State	
Disturbing School	49 cases	Assault & Battery 3rd degree	2,522 cases
Assault & Battery 3rd degree	38 cases	Shoplifting (up to $1,000)	1,354 cases
Incorrigibility	25 cases	Disturbing School	1,101 cases
Shoplifting (up to $1,000)	19 case(s)	Public Disorderly Conduct	1,082 cases
Simple Possession of Marijuana	16 case(s)	Simple Possession of Marijuana	877 cases

Rate of Delinquency Processing for Age-Eligible Juveniles

	County	State
Number of Juveniles Ages 10 - 16 years (2010 Census)	10,503	418,739
Percent of Age-Eligible Population	3%	4%
Rate per 1,000 Age-Eligible Juveniles	26	40

Social Characteristics of Juvenile Referrals*

Race:	County	State	Age:	County	State
Black	71%	57%	13 years and younger	17%	21%
White	27%	39%	14 and 15 years	46%	44%
Hispanic	0%	3%	16 years and older	36%	35%
Other	1%	1%			
Sex:					
Male	70%	70%			
Female	30%	30%			

Court Processing and Disposition of Juvenile Referrals*

Solicitor Action:	County	State	Judicial Disposition:	County	State
Dismiss or Divert	63%	55%	Dismiss or Acquit	5%	5%
Prosecute/Issue Rule	37%	44%	School Order	0%	7%
Other:	0%	0%	Probation	65%	59%
			Commitment	28%	25%
			Other	1%	4%
Pre- Dispositional Evaluations:					
			Commitments to DJJ:		
Community Evaluation	16%	42%	Evaluation Commitments	26	1,329
Residential Evaluation	84%	58%	Final Commitments	21	1,374

South Carolina Department of Juvenile Justice
Office of Planning and Programs
Research and Statistics Section
Telephone (803) 896-7538

* Some percentages do not
add to 100% due to rounding

Appendix 8: George Stinney Jr. of Alcolu, SC

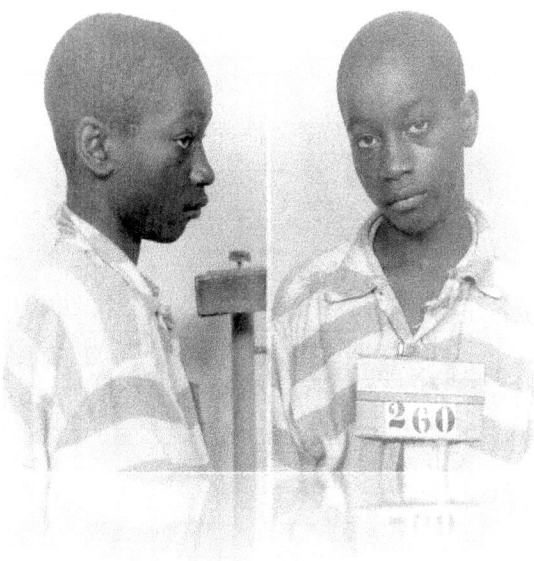

Source: Public Domain Image from State of South Carolina (1944). *George Stinney mugshot.*
Retrieved from http://commons.wikimedia.org/wiki/File:George _Stinney_mugshot.jpg

Appendix 9: SCDOC Profile of Inmates

South Carolina Department of Corrections
Profile of Inmates in Institutional Count
(Including Inmates on Authorized Absence) as of June 30, 2013

Characteristics	Male Population		Female Population		Total Population	
TOTAL Inmates Population	**20,777**		**1,391**		**22,168**	
	#	%	#	%	#	%
Current Age						
Average Current Age	36.6		37.6		36.7	
21 & Under	1,321	6%	46	3%	1,367	6%
22-25	2,756	13%	135	10%	2,891	13%
26-35	6,939	33%	460	33%	7,399	33%
36-55	8,164	39%	675	49%	8,839	40%
56 and Over	1,597	8%	75	5%	1,672	8%
Average Age at Admission	31.2		34.1		31.4	
Race						
Black	13,631	66%	556	40%	14,187	64%
White	6,599	32%	802	58%	7,401	33%
Other	547	3%	33	2%	580	3%
Citizenship						
Illegal Aliens	468	2%	19	1%	487	2%
Citizens	20,309	98%	1372	99%	21,681	98%
Marital Status (Self-reported)						
Single	12,904	62%	645	46%	13,549	61%
Married	6,156	30%	562	40%	6,718	30%
Divorced	1,461	7%	131	9%	1,592	7%
Widowed	256	1%	53	4%	309	1%
Sentencing Data/Criminal History						
Admission Type:						
New	16,553	80%	1230	88%	17,783	80%
Revocator	4,000	19%	157	11%	4,157	19%
Other	224	1%	4	0.3%	228	1%
With Current Violent Offense	13,260	64%	675	49%	13,935	63%
With Prior Criminal History	12,952	62%	630	45%	13,582	61%
With Prior Commitments	9,250	45%	407	29%	9,657	44%
Average Sentence Length in Years	13.9		9.3		13.6	
Average Time to Serve before Maxout	5.9		4.0		5.8	
Sentences One Year or Less (excl. YOA)	649	3%	128	9%	777	4%
Sentences More than 20 years (excl lifers)	3,185	15%	132	9%	3,317	15%
With Life Sentence	2,120	10%	85	6%	2,205	10%
With YOA/Juvenile Sentence	802	4%	25	2%	827	4%
On Death Row	47	0.2%	0	0%	47	0.2%
Non-Parolable (includes TIS inmates)	10,880	52%	541	00%	11,415	51%
TIS Sentences	10,593	51%	540	39%	11,133	50%
Special Needs						
With Children	13,557	65%	1,094	79%	14,651	66%
With Convicted Disciplinaries in Last 12 Months	7,416	36%	254	18%	7,670	35%
With Victim Witness Indicator	12,567	60%	716	51%	13,283	60%
Sex Registry	3,373	16%	41	3%	3,414	15%
Required DNA Testing	20,393	98%	1,288	93%	21,681	98%
Chemical Dependent per SASSI/TCUDDS	7,696	37%	752	54%	8,448	38%
Education/Work						
Average (Latest) Reading Score	8.7		9.9		8.8	
Reading Score is <12th Grade	15,050	72%	837	60%	15,887	72%
Reading Score is <9th Grade	10,082	49%	464	33%	10,546	48%
Average Education Level at Intake	10.5		11.0		10.5	
Without HS/GED	11,518	55%	620	45%	12,138	55%

Appendix 10: Examples of Correctional Offense Codes

SOUTH CAROLINA DEPARTMENT OF CORRECTIONS
OFFENSE CODES

OFFENSE CODE	OFFENSE DESCRIPTION	OFFENSE CATEGORY
0027	DRUG CONSP/ATT.TO VIOLA	2
0256	RESIST ARREST/ASSLT OFF.	4
0368	TRAFFICK METH 100GR MORE	4
0389	TRAFFICK METH 28-100GR 2	4
0392	TRAFFICK METH 28-100GR 1	4
0450	TRAFFICK METH 10-28GR 1	4
0451	TRAFFICK METH 10-28GR 2	4
0452	TRAFFICK METH DAY FOR DY	4
0461	SEX W/INM/PAT.MENTAL FAC	3
0497	TAMPER W/VIDEO GAME MACH	1
0531	OBTAIN SIG/FRAUD $1K-$5K	1
0615	WEAPONS ON SCHOOL PROPER	3
0912	LYNCHING-2ND DEGREE	3
0913	INVOLUNTARY MANSLAUGHTER	3
0914	MANSLAUGHTER BEFOR 6/3/8	4
0916	RECKLESS HOMICIDE	3
0917	LYNCHING 1ST DEGREE	4
0918	KILLING IN A DUEL	4
0919	VOLUNTARY MANSLAUGHTER	4
0922	ADMINISTERING POISON	3
0923	HOMICIDE BY CHILD ABUSE	5
0924	ADMIN POISON W/INT KILL	4
0925	KILL BY STABBING/THRUSTI	5
0989	MURDER BEFORE 1977, JUNE	5
0999	MURDER	5
1000	KIDNAPPING	5
1012	TAKING HOSTAGES BY INMAT	5
1013	FALSE IMPRISONMENT	4

Appendix 11: Examples of School Offense Codes

Category I Offenses
- Aggravated Assault
- Alcohol/Liquor Law Violation
- Arson
- Bomb Threat
- Bribery
- Burglary
- Computer Violation
- Contraband
- Contract Violation
- Disturbing School
- Drug Distribution
- Drug Possession
- Drug Violation
- Embezzlement
- Extortion
- Fire Alarm
- Fireworks
- Forced Sexual Offense
- Fraud
- Gang Activity
- Harassment
- Indecent Exposure
- Intimidation
- Kidnap/Abduction
- Non-forcible Sexual Offense
- Other Offense
- Pornography
- Probation Violation
- Prostitution
- Robbery
- Sexual Harassment
- Simple Assault
- Threat
- Vehicle Theft
- Weapons

Category I Actions – Grades Pre-K - 12
* Referral to the hearing officer
* Suspension until the hearing before the hearing officer which is usually scheduled within 10 school days and no more than 5 school days after parent notification
* See administration actions addendum

Special Education Students: Notify District Psychologist
* See Discipline for Student with an Identified Disability Addendum
* See Administrative Actions Addendum

Category II Offenses
- Bite/Pinch/Spit
- Bullying*
- Computer Violation
- Contraband
- Cyber bullying
- Driving Violation
- Fighting*
- Fireworks
- Forgery
- Gang Activity*

Appendix 12: Construct, USA's Website Constituency

Demographics

- 100% are low-income
- 94% enter without a high school diploma
- 71% are men; 29% are women
- 53% are African American; 22% are White; 20% are Latino; 3% are Native American; 2% are Asian American
- 32% are court-involved
- 45% have received public assistance

Appendix 13: Case and Hunter

Table 1 Challenging processes, specific mechanisms, and effects

Challenging processes	Specific mechanisms	Effects
Narrative identity work	Creation/maintenance of:	
	Oppression narratives	Affirm and privilege the individual's subjective experience of oppression
	Resistance narratives	Ready the individual to respond to oppression; embody the individual's right to respect and dignity; provide a vision of an alternative future, and instill a sense of hope concerning a better tomorrow; prevent internalized oppression
	Reimagined personal narratives	Re-craft individual identities which have been misrepresented and demeaned through dominant cultural narratives
Acts of resistance	Collective critique Engaging in non-normative behaviors	Act out and thus enhance resistance and reimagined personal narratives; act out and celebrate aspects of the individual's culture and identity that are devalued within the larger society
Direct relational transactions	Fostering empathy and security through a shared sense of community	Amelioration of current psychological distress and feelings of isolation and exclusion
	Transmission of adaptive cognitive and behavioral strategies for responding to oppression	Enhancement of self-protective mechanisms

www.ingramcontent.com/pod-product-compliance
Lightning Source LLC
Chambersburg PA
CBHW070535290526
45790CB00002B/506